William Henry Pearson

List of Canadian Hepaticæ

William Henry Pearson

List of Canadian Hepaticæ

ISBN/EAN: 9783337186739

Printed in Europe, USA, Canada, Australia, Japan

Cover: Foto ©ninafisch / pixelio.de

More available books at **www.hansebooks.com**

GEOLOGICAL AND NATURAL HISTORY SURVEY OF CANADA
ALFRED R. C. SELWYN, C.M.G., LL.D., F.R.S., &c., DIRECTOR.

LIST

OF

CANADIAN HEPATICÆ

BY

WM. HY. PEARSON.

MONTREAL:

WM. FOSTER BROWN & CO.

1890.

PREFACE.

The following list is the result of the microscopical examination of a large collection of Hepaticæ made by Mr. Macoun in different parts of Canada, and of those in my possession from the herbarium of the late Mr. Austin; in order to make the list as complete as possible I have added all records known to me of species found in Canada and northwards, including those mentioned in G. L. N. Syn. Hep. (1884); Mitten, The "Bryologia" of the Survey of the 49th Parallel of Latitude, Pro. Linn. Soc., Vol. VIII. (1846); Stephani Hepaticæ von der Halbinsel Alaska, Bot. Jahr., Vol. VIII. (1886) and Delâmare, Renauld et Cardot's "Flora Miquelonsis" (1888) (Hepaticæ determined by Stephani.)

The striking feature of the flora is its great similarity to that of Northern Europe, as Dr. Spruce intimated in his note on *Arnellia fennica.*

In my descriptions I have adopted the terms used by Dr. Spruce in his monograph "On Cephalozia" 1882.)

WM. HY. PEARSON.

ECCLES, ENGLAND.

LIST OF CANADIAN HEPATICÆ.

By W. H. Pearson.

Frullania Selwyniana, n. sp.

Small, reddish brown, irregularly dichotomously branched, innovant branches produced repeatedly from below the female bracts. Leaves imbricate, rotund, slightly papillose, with lines of moniliform cells; lobule ⅓th smaller than the leaf, galeate, wide mouth, erect or a little divergent from the stem; stylus wanting or very minute; cells small to rather minute. Underleaves about ¼ smaller than the leaves, rather broader than the stem, oval, to a ¼ acutely bifid, segments acutate, slightly unidentate. Inflorescence monoicous, terminal on short branches. Bracts 3 pairs, the innermost about twice the size of the leaves, unequally lobed, complicate, lobe obtusate, irregularly dentate-serrate; lobule acute with a large segment near the middle, margin distantly ciliate-dentate; second bracts similar, only smaller and less dentate; third bracts subentire. Bracteole free, bifid to below the middle, sinus and segments acute, margin ciliate-dentate. Perianth small, submersed, pyriform, smooth, trigonous, antical face plane, postical broadly carinate, apex rostellate. Male bracts 3 pairs, on short lateral branches immediately below the female, globose.

Hab.—On trees, Ste. Anne's River, Gaspé, 19th August, 1882. (*Macoun*.)

Obs.—I take the pleasure of naming this distinct and beautiful little species in honor of Dr. Selwyn, C.M.G., the able and distinguished Director of the Geological and Natural History Department of Canada, under whose auspices this list is published. It differs from *Frullania polysticta Lindenb* in the absence of the large irregularly interposed cells, in the lobule of the bracts being much smaller than the lobe (not of equal size), and in the margin of the under leaves being uni-dentate near the middle, from *Frullania fragilifolia* Tayl. in being monoicous, and in the irregularly ciliate-dentate lobule of the bracts, which has a large segment near the middle.

Measurements.—Fronds ½ to ¾ inch long, ·5 to ·75 mm. wide, stem ·1 m. diam., leaves ·4 mm. long x ·3 mm. broad, ·3 mm. x ·25 mm., lobule ·15 mm. high x ·1 mm. broad, cells ·02 mm. x ·015 mm. ·015 mm. x ·015 n.m., underleaves ·175 mm. long x ·15 mm. broad, sinus ·05 mm., ·2 mm. x .175 mm., sinus ·05, ·25 x ·15 mm., lobule ·45 mm. long x ·225 mm. broad at the base of the juncture, bract lobe ·75 mm. long x ·4 mm. broad, lobule ·6 mm. long x ·25 mm. broad, ·85 mm. x ·35 mm. lobule ·75 mm. x ·45 mm.

Description of Pl 1.—Fig. 1. Plants nat. size. 2. Plant x 24, an-tical view. 3. Portion of stem x 64, postical view. 4. Portion of leaf x 290. 5-7. Underleaves x 64. 8. Bract x 64. 9. Bract x 31. 10. Second bract x 64. 11. Bracteole x 31. 12. Perianth x 31. 13. Cross-section of the perianth x 31.

2. Frullania Virginica, Gottsch.

Hab.—New Brunswick. (*James, Herb. Austin, cum per.*) Hastings Co., Ont., May, 1868. (*Macoun, Herb. Austin.*)

3. Frullania Hallii, Aust. Bull. Torrey Bot. Club, 6, n. 2, 1875.

Hab.—On trees, Vancouver Island, May, 1875. (*Macoun.*)

4. Frullania Eboracensis, Gottsch.

Hab.—On trees, at Belleville, Ont., 1868 (18-35). On fir trees in woods, Gaspé, 1882 (8). On birch trees, Ste. Anne's River, Gaspé, ♂ et ♀ *cum per.*, August, 1882 (12). Ottawa, 1883, *cum per.* (246-228-252). On birch trees, Truro, Nova Scotia, June, 1883 (172). On rocks, Lake Nipigon, July, 1884 (9). On poplar bark, Vancouver Island, May, 1887 (22). On rocks, V. I., May, 1887 (228). (*Macoun.*)

Obs.—Several forms are in the collection, but as the characters are more or less variable in the different organs on the same stems, I have not thought them worthy of ranking even as varieties. In the draw-ings taken under the prism are given several figures showing this.

In one compact form the perianths were often more rotund with the lobule of the bract obtusate (fig. 8-9-10), in another, the perianth was slightly keeled antically (fig. 17), and almost bicarinate postically (fig. 16-17), and some lobules of the bracts uni-bidentate at the base (fig. 14).

Description of Pl. II.—Fig. 1. Portion of stem x **31** (8.) **2.** Under-leaf x (8). 3-4. Bracts x 31 (8). **5.** Bracteole x (8). 6. Perianth **x** (8). 7. Cross-section of the perianth x (8). 8. Bract x **31** (11). **9.** Bracteole x 64 (11). 10. Perianth x 31 (11). 11-12. Underleaves **x** 85 (9). 13-14. Bracts **x** 31 (9). 15. Bracteole x 31- 16-17. Cross-section of the perianth x 31 (9). **18.** Bract x 31 (**172**). **19.** Bracteole **x** 31 (12).

5. Frullania Tamarisci, (L.) Radd.

Hab.—" Vancouver Island and Orcas Island. Collected also by *Menzies* and *Douglas* on the N. W. coast. The specimens are very slender, and at first sight would scarcely be supposed to belong to the same species as the European forms; the leaves are rounded, in the fertile stems acute, in the male plants with the point inflexed and the colored cells in some of the leaves are only found after careful search. No American examples have yet been met with which can compare with the British in size." (*Mitt.*) Miquelon Island. (*Delàmare.*)

6. Frullania Asagrayana, Mont.

Hab.—On rocks on an island in Gull Lake, Victoria Co., Ont., July, 1868 (32). (*Macoun.*) Charlottetown, Prince Edward Island. (*James.*) Bass River, New Brunswick, 1871. (*J. Fowler.*) On birch trees, coast of Gaspé, August, 1882 (7). (*Macoun.*) Island of Miquelon. (*Delàmare.*)

7. Frullania Asagrayana, Mont. var.

Hab.—On rocks, Pirate's Cove, Nova Scotia, 1883 (111). (*Macoun.*) On rocks, Vancouver Island, 1885 (139). On trees, V. I., 1885 (140) (*Dawson.*)

8. Frullania Asagrayana, Mont. var. Californica. Aust. MS. Underw. Catal., Hep. N. Amer., p. 67, 1883.

Hab.—On rotten wood, Nanaimo, Vancouver Island, 4th June, 1887 (86). On trees in woods, Comox, V. I., 29th July, 1887 (57). (*Macoun.*)

9. Frullania Nisquallensis, Sulliv. Mem. Amer. Acad. N. Ser. III. p. 175.

Hab.—On the bark of cedars, Mount Mark, 26th July, 1887 (102). ♂ and young ♀ Vancouver Island, 26th May, 1887 (22). (*Macoun.*) Alaska. (*Krause.*)

Description of Pl. III.—Figs. 1-2. **Bracts x 31 (139)**. 3. Bracteole **x** 31 (139). 4. Second bracteole **x** 31 (139). 5. Perianth x 16 (139). 6. Cross-section of **the** same x 16. 7. Bracteole **x 31** (140). 8. Second bracteole x 31 **(140)**. 9. Cross-section of perianth **x** 31 (140).

10. **Frullania Chilcootiensis,** Steph.

Alaska. (*Krause.*)

11. **Radula complanata,** (L.) Nees.

Hab.—On trees, Ste. Anne's River, Gaspé, 22nd Aug., 1884 (15). On rocks, Ottawa, 1885 (129). On the base of trees, Nanaimo, **Vancouver** Island, 4th June, 1887 (85). (*Macoun.*) British Columbia. (*Lyall.*) "A few fragments only." (*Mitt.*) Island of Miquelon. (*Delàmare.*)

12. **Radula commutata,** Gottsche.

I picked out from some other species a sterile gemmiparous *Radula*, which will probably be this. Hab.—On rocks, on the banks of the Moira, Belleville, 1865. (*Macoun.*)

13. **Radula tenax,** Lindb.

Hab. On the bark of trees, Vancouver Island, 1885 (146). (*Dawson.*)

14. **Radula Krausei,** Steph.

Alaska. (*Krause.*)

15. **Radula arctica,** Steph.

Alaska. (*Krause.*)

16. **Radula spicata,** Aust. Bull. Torrey Bot. Club, 6, N. 3, 1875. *Radula Bolanderi* Gottsche. "Steph. 'Hedwigia,' N. 10, 1884."

Hab.—On rotten wood, Vancouver Island, 1885 (162.) (*Dawson.*)

Obs.—Mr. Mitten published prior to Austin a *Radula spicata* ("Bonplandia," 1862), but according to Stephani this is synonymous with *Radula formosa* (Meissn.). Nees (1827). Gottsche, not aware of the *Radula* of Austin, took drawings of it and named it *Radula Bolanderi*, under which name it was published by Stephani. I add the following interesting letter from Herr Stephani with reference to the matter:

"Mr. Mitten lent me his *Radulæ.* I had no permission to keep them, and it was so very little that I could not well even take off a leaf for the sake of the form and the texture; but I have made careful drawings and I am *absolutely sure* that his *R. spicata* is the same as *R. formosa*. In my notes I have put down that it is not even a form but altogether corresponds to the original plant of Nees, of which I enclose a specimen to keep. When I wrote the article on *Radula*, I was not aware that Austin had published a plant, which he called *R. spicata*. Some years later I got the book of Mr. Underwood, who gives an enumeration of all the known American Hepaticæ. I at once recognized the *R. spicata* Austin, named in this book (with Austin's description) to be Gottsche's *Radula Bolanderi*, and so your specimens prove it to be. I have described this plant on page 12 of my article on *Radulæ*. I suppose Mr. Austin has the priority, and as the name of Mitten must fall, Austin's name of *Radula spicata* has to stand for *R. Bolanderi*, G., who knew it long before Austin recognized this plant, but never published a description of it; he got the plant from Mr. Bolander of San Francisco, and I have got it from Gottsche and from numerous other localities of Western and Southern United States."

Description of Pl. IV.—Fig. 1. Plants natural size. 2-3. Portions of stems with perianths, x 24. 4. Portions of stem with ♂ spike, x 24.

17. Lejeunea serpyllifolia, (Dicks.) Libert.

Hab.—On moss and rocks along the Moira, Belleville, 1865. On cedar trees, Ste. Anne's River, Gaspé, 19th Aug., 1882. (*Macoun.*) Island of Miquelon. (*Delamare.*)

Var. Americana, Lindb.

Hab.—On earth along the Moira River at Belleville, Ont. (*Macoun.*)

18. Lejeunea Biddlecomiæ, Aust. MSS.

Hab.—On trees, Canada. (*Macoun, Herb. Aust.*)

Obs.—I add some interesting notes by Dr. Spruce:—

"As to *Lejeunea Biddlecomiæ*, when I first examined it, I hoped it might be kept apart from *L. calcarea* by the much wider leaves; but I have lately gone over these plants and their exotic allies, and I find European forms of *L. calcarea* scarcely distinguishable from the American plant. When I first noticed the styliform appendage to the leaves, I took it to be a unicrural (one-legged) stipule; but as I could never find the other leg, I afterwards held it (with Lindberg) to be a special organ, and placed it in *Cololejeunea*. Careful study of all the *Drepano-*

lejuneæ has now convinced me that my first impression was right, and that *L. calcarea* is really a near ally of *L. hamatifolia*, etc.; for, in many of these, it is not uncommon to find one leg wanting to the stipule, and the remaining leg connate with the base of the adjacent leaf, exactly as in *L. calcarea.* I enclose my notes on *Lejeunea Biddlecomiæ,* of which you may use what you like." (*R. Spruce,* 1888.)

Lejeunea Biddlecomiæ, Aust.—*L. calcarea var.,* Florida. On rotting wood. (*Miss Biddlecome.*)

Closely allied to *Drepano-Lejeunea calcarea,* but twice the size. Leaves more dimidiate, semi-ovate-lanceolate, postical margin straight or sub-concave, surface less sharply muriculate, margins often merely crenulate (from the cells being obtuse, not acute), or muricato-serrulate only at keel and point; *lobule only* ⅓ (not ½) of leaf; *stylus* longer (6-8 cells long), often so erect and appressed to the stem as to escape notice, but sometimes really obsolete.

Perianth, much like that of *L. calcarea,* but not so rough.
♀ *Bracts* variable, when expanded broader than long.

Antheridia solitary in axils of a few upper leaves of a branch; these leaves (or bracts) have a proportionately much larger lobule than stem-leaves, but are still far from equilobed.

Note.—The stylus is probably a unicrural stipule, very slightly connate at base to adjacent leaf. (*R. Spruce,* 1884.)

" Such is doubtless its true character, and it proves *L. calcarea* to be a congener of *L. hamatifolia, i.e.,* a *Drepanolejeunea,* not a *Cololejeunea,* as I had considered it in Hep. A. A. I long ago noted that one leg of a bipartite (or two-legged) stipule was sometimes wanting, both in *Drepanolejeunea* and *Leptolejeunea (elliptica,* etc.) Others have noted the same thing. (*See Syn. Hep*) 344 *Lej. hamatifolia, β* & *γ*: " Stipule of 2 minute divergent crura, each 2 cells long. Sometimes the stipules are simply subulate." Also of *L. dactylophora*: "Stipules subulate, lower bifid, upper entire. I have a fine patch of *L. calcarea,* gathered in the Ardennes by Mme. Libert herself; it cannot (I think) be specifically separated from *L. Biddlecomiæ.*" (*R. S.,* 1888.)

Description of Pl. V.—Fig. 1. Portion of stem, antical view, x 64. 2. Portion of stem, postical view, x 64. 3-8. Leaves x 85. 9. Portion of leaf x 290. 10. Styli x 85. 11, 12. Bracts x 85. 13. Bracteole x 85. 14. Antheridia x 85.

19. **Porella navicularis,** (L. et L.) Dill.

Hab.—Observatory Inlet, British Columbia. (*Dr. Scouler, Herb.*

Torrey.) Vancouver Island, 23rd December, 1872 (43). On trees, V. I., 6th May, 1875 (15). (*Macoun*). On trees, V. I., 1885 (141). (*Dawson.*) On trees, V. I., ♂ and ♀ with perianth, 9th May, 1887 (21). On trees, Comox, V. I., 27th April, 1887 (54). (*Macoun.*) Vancouver Island and near Fort Colville. (*Lyall.*) Alaska. (*Krause.*)

20. Porella **platyphylloidea,** (Schweintz.)

Hab.—On trees, Vancouver Island, 9th May, 1887 (19). (*Macoun.*) These specimens agree in every particular with original ones from Schweintz. Fort Colville. (*Lyall.*)

21. Porella **laevigata,** (Nees.)

Hab.—Kettle Falls, Columbia River. (*Lyall. in Herb. Mitt.*) On rocks, Fraser Canyon, above Yale, B.C., 1875 (*Macoun.*)

22. Porella **platyphylla,** (L.)

Hab.—Unalaschka, Chamisso in Hb. Acad. Petropolit. Hb. Mont., n. 206, var. β., *major convexula.* (*Syn. Hep.* 279.) Alaska. (*Krause.*)

23. Porella **rivularis,** (Nees.)

Hab.—On trees, along the Fraser River, 1872. (*Macoun, Hb. Aust.*)

24. Porella **Bolanderi** (Aust.) Bull. Torrey Bot. Club, 3, p. 84.

Hab.—On rocks, Nanaimo River, Vancouver Island, 26th April, 1887 (59). On rocks, Cedar Hill, V.I., 9th May, 1887 (18). (*Macoun.*)

25. Porella **Bolanderi,** (Aust.) var.

Mount Benson alt. 3,000 ft., Vancouver Island, 8th June, 1887 (77). (*Macoun.*)

26. **Ptilidium Californicum,** (Aust.) Pearson. (*Mastigophora Californica* Aust.) (*Lepidozia Californica* Aust.) Bull. Torrey Bot. Club, 6, 19, 302, 1875.

Hab.—On old logs, Comox, Vancouver Island, 29th April, 1887 (73). (*Macoun.*) Vancouver Island, 1875. (*Macoun, Herb. Austin.*)

Obs.—Having met with perianths of this beautiful species I have no hesitation in referring it to *Ptilidium.*

27. Ptilidium pulcherrimum, (Web.) Nees.

Hab.—On logs, Gaspé, Q., 10th August, 1882. (*Macoun.*)

28. Ptilidium ciliare, (L.) Nees.

Hab.—On earth and logs, Gaspé coast, Q., 10th August, 1882 (18).
Peat bog, Anticosti, 1883 (104). On the perpendicular face of rocks,
Lake Nipigon, Ontario, 10th July, 1884 (63a). On rocks, in the
Rocky Mountains, 29th July, 1885 (143). (*Macoun.*) Alaska.
(*Krause.*) Greenland. (*Syn. Hep.* p. 251.) Fort Colville. (*Lyall.*)
Miquelon Island. (*Delàmare.*) Nottingham Island, Hudson Strait,
1883 (109). (*Dr. Bell.*)

29. Lepidozia reptans, (L.) Dum.

Hab.—House Mts., Little Slave Lake, 1872 (193a). On old logs,
Ste. Anne's River, Gaspé, 18th August, 1882 (20). Ottawa, 1883
(237a). On dead wood, in the Rocky Mountains, 21st July, 1885
(144). On trees, at their base. On rotten wood, Comox, Vancouver
Island, 29th, 30th April, 1887 (66, 67). On rotten logs, V.I., 19th
May, 1887. (*Macoun.*) Fort Colville. (*Lyall.*) Miquelon Island.
(*Delàmare.*) Vancouver Island, 1885 (145). (*Dawson.*)

30. Lepidozia setacea, (Web.) Mitt.

Hab.—Miquelon Island. (*Delàmare.*)

31. Trichocolea tomentella, (Ehrb.) Dum.

Hab.—Miquelon Island. (*Delamare.*) Common in tamarack swamps,
Ontario. (*Macoun.*)

32. Bazzania deflexa, (Nees.) B. Gray.

Hab.—On rotten wood, Vancouver Island, 1885 (164). (*Dawson.*)
On earth, at Comox, V.I., May, 1887 (39). (*Macoun.*) Alaska.
(*Krause.*) British Columbia. (*Lyall*), as *Mastigobrum ambiguum* by
Mitten. (*Bazzania ambigua Lindenb.* according to Austin, is to be
referred to this species "Steph." Hedwigia, 1886.)

33. Bazzania trilobata, (L.) B. Gray.

Hab.—Newfoundland, collected by a French sea captain (*Hb.
Le Jolis*). On old logs and stumps, Gaspé coast, 2nd August, 1882
(19). On rocks, at Truro, Nova Scotia, 1883 (176). (*Macoun.*)

34. Bazzania denudata, (Torrey.) B. Gray.

Hab.—Miquelon Island. (Delàmare.) This species is also referred to *Bazzania deflexa* N., by Austin. (Aust. Hep. Bor. Amer., p. 20.)

35. Cephalozia (Eucephalozia) catenulata, (Hüben.)

Hab.—On old logs, at Belleville, 1869 (199a). Lake Superior, 1869 (256). On rotten logs, British Columbia, 1872 (209). On old logs, Peace River, B.C., 1872 (195). B. C., 1875 (242). On old logs, Gaspé, 2nd August, 1882 (30). On rotten logs, Gaspé, 17th August, 1882 (31). Ottawa, 1883 (250). On rotten wood, Truro, Nova Scotia, 1883 (179). On burnt wood, Sudbury Junction, 28th May, 1884 (72). Vancouver Island, May, 1887 (4, 8, 12, 16, 20). (Macoun.) Miquelon Island. (Delàmare.)

36. Cephalozia (Eucephalozia) multiflora, Spruce.

Hab.—On rotten wood, British Columbia, 1875 (208). St. Mary's River, Anticosti, 1883 (123). On earth, in a swamp at Nipigon, Lake Superior, June, 1884 (69). On rotten wood, very common, July, 1885 (152). (Macoun.) Miquelon Island. (Delàmare.)

37. Cephalozia (Eucephalozia) pleniceps, (Aust.) Proc. Ac. Nat. Sc. Philad. 1869. (*Cephalozia crassiflora.* Spruce.)

Hab.—On rotten wood, Ottawa, 1884 (70). On earth and rocks, Ottawa, 1884 (80). On *Sphagnum*, close to the snow, Rocky Mountains; alt., 7,500 ft., July 22, 1885 (151). On old logs, Nanaimo, Vancouver Island, 6th June, 1887 (47). (Macoun).

Obs. Dr. Spruce in his admirable monograph, "On Cephalozia," surmises that his *Ceph. crassiflora* may be the same as Austin's *C. pleniceps*, and from the examination of a number of specimens, I arrive at the opinion that they are the same species.

38. Cephalozia (Eucephalozia) bicuspidata, (L.) Dum.

Hab.—Jupiter River, Anticosti, 1883 (128). (Macoun.) Greenland. (*Vahl. Syn. Hep.* p. 140). Rocky Mountains. (*Lyall.*) Peat swamps, at Belleville, Ont. (*Macoun, Austin Herb.*) Miquelon Island. (*Delàmare.*)

39. Cephalozia (Eucephalozia) Lammersiana, (Hüben). S.

Hab.—On rotten logs, Selkirk Mountains, B.C., July, 1885 (153) (Macoun.)

40. Cephalozia (Eucephalozia) extensa, (Tayl.) Spruce.

Hab.—On rotten wood and earth, Comox, Vancouver Island, April, May, 1887 (5, 33, 37, 38, 42, 44, 52, 53, 55, 58, 61, 65, 69, 71, 74).

41. Cephalozia (Eucephalozia) curvifolia, (Dicks.) Dum.

Hab.—On logs, Belleville, 1882 (230a). On rotten wood, Ste. Anne's River, Gaspé, 22nd August, 1882 (32), *cum per.* On rotten wood, Ottawa, 1885 (131). (*Macoun.*)

42. Cephalozia (Eucephalozia) fluitans, (Nees.) Spruce.

Hab.—Salt Lake, Anticosti, 1883 (118). (*Macoun.*) Canada as *Cephalozia Francisci* var. *fluitans*, (*Austin*), Miquelon Island (*Delàmare*), as *Jungermania fluitans, Lindb.*, and new to America (1887), it is the *Cephalozia obtusiloba*, of *Lindb.*, and is recorded as *Cephalozia Francisci* var. *fluitans*, by Underwood. " Cat. North Amer. Hep. p. 96, 1883."

43. Cephalozia (Odontoschisma) Sphagni, (Dicks.) Spruce.

Hab.—Miquelon Island. (*Delàmare.*) On logs, at Belleville, Ont. (*Macoun.*)

44. Cephalozia (Odontoschisma) denudata, (Mart.) Spruce.

Hab.—Ottawa, 1883 (245). (*Macoun.*) Miquelon Island. (*Delàmare.*)

45. Cephalozia (Odontoschisma) Austini, Pears. MSS.

Odontoschisma Macounii, Aust., in Bull. Torrey Bot. Club, 3, 13, 187.

Hab.—On damp ground north shore of Lake Superior, Canada. (*Macoun.*)

Obs.—As Dr. Spruce unites *Odontoschisma* with *Cephalozia*, and there is a *Cephalozia Macounii*, I have, with Mr. Macoun's approval, attached the name of the late C. F. Austin to it, as suggested by Dr. Spruce.

46. Cephalozia (Cephaloziella) divaricata, (Sm.) Dum.

Hab.—On earth, Vancouver Island, *cum per.*, 1875 (198). Yarmouth, Nova Scotia, 1883 (125). On rocks, Sudbury Junction, 28th May, 1884 (84). On rocks, Nipigon River, 6th July, 1884 (81). (*Macoun.*) Greenland. (*Vahl. Syn. Hep.* p. 136.) Cascade Mountains, British Columbia. (*Lyall.*)

47. **Cephalozia** (Cephaloziella) **Macounii,** Aust. Hep. Bor. Amer. 1873, *Jung. Macounii* Aust. in Proc. Ac. Nat. Sc. Philad. 1869.

"*Dioica* cladocarpa eflagellifera; *caule* tenui pellucido flexuoso radicelloso crebrius ramoso. *Folia* viridia, contigua vel subimbricata, late patentia cuneata parum complicato-carinata, ad vel paulo ultra ½ bifida, sinu lato obtusato lunatove, lobis patulis subdivergentibus late subulatis (basi 2-4 cell. latis) pro more acutis; *cellulis* parvis subquadratis subpellucidis. *Foliola* O. *Bracteæ* ♀ 2-3 jugæ tristichæ appressæ liberæ vel subconnatæ, vix ad ½ usque 2-3 lobæ irregulariter spinulosæ. *Perianthia parvula* albida leptodermia, obovato-vel-ovato-fusiformia, obtuse trigona, ore subconstricto setuloso ciliolatove. *Andraecia* caulis ramive apicem mediumve tenentia.

Measurements—F. .15 x .10, per .75 x .25 mm." R. Spruce, "On Cephalozia," p. 68.

Hab.—On rotting wood, near Belleville, Ont., 1865, 1867, 1870. (*Macoun.*)

48. **Cephalozia** (Cephaloziella) **Sullivantii,** (Aust.) Spruce.

(*Jung. divaricata* Sulliv. Musc. Allegh. 239; on rotten wood in Canada) "quoad habitum et minutiem *C. micromeræ* nostræ persimilis, et cellulis autem præminutis et perianthiis ore haud 6-laciniatis longe aliena *Cephaloziella* vera videretur *C. Macounii* affinis sed longe minor et stipulifera mihi tamen solum e specimenibus mancis male cognita." R. Spruce, "On Cephalozia," p. 68,

Hab.—On rotten elm logs, in swamps at Belleville, Ont. (*Macoun.*)

49. **Cephalozia** (Prionolobus) **minima,** Austin MSS.

Dioicous, acrocarpous, green, eflagelliferous, minute. Stems thick, short, simple, capitate, 5 cells in diameter, cortical cells 10-15-seriate. Leaves obovate, broadly ovate or sub-quadrate, sub-carinate, margin quite entire, upper leaves larger, crowded, bifid to ⅓, segments acute or acutate, broad or narrow. Cells 4-6 sided, very minute, (.016 mm.), trigones wanting, walls moderately thick. Underleaves everywhere present, lower ones entire, broadly subulate; upper larger, bifid, segments subulate. Bracts 3 pairs, larger than the leaves, subquadrate, bilobed down to ⅓-½, spinulose-dentate with a large tooth near the base on each side; bracteoles similar, only smaller. Perianth oblong-oval, composed of a single layer of cells, mouth rather wide, sub-entire.

Male stems more slender, with the antheridia on short postical branches, antheridia 3-4, solitary, very small, roundish.

Obs—Near *Cephalozia dentata*, (Raddi) but differs from it in the entire stem leaves, in addition to other characters.

Hab.—Grows on rotten wood and old logs, Belleville, Ont., 1868. (*Macoun, IIb. Austin.*)

Measurements—Stems 1-2 mm. long, .3 mm. diam., leaves .15 mm. long x .1 mm. broad, seg. .05 mm., .15 mm. long x .1 mm. broad; seg. .075 mm., .125 mm. long x .1 mm. broad, seg. .05 mm.; cells .0167 mm.; upper underleaves .1 mm. long x .06 mm. broad; seg. .05; innermost bract .25 mm. x .3 mm., seg. .125 mm., .225 mm. x .3 mm., seg. .1 mm.; 2nd bract .225 mm. x .175 mm., seg. .1 mm.; bracteole .175 mm. long x .175 mm. broad; seg. .125 mm., pistillidia .075 mm .x .03; antheridia .04 mm.

Description of Pl. VI.—Fig. 1. Plants nat. size. 2. Young stem x 85. 3-12. Leaves x 85. 13. Portion of leaf x 290. 14-16. Folioles magnified. 17. Upper foliole x 85. 18. Innermost bracts and bracteole x 85. 19. Innermost bract x 85. 20. 2nd bracts and bracteole x 85. 21. 2nd bracts x 85. 22. 3rd bracts x 85. 23. Pistillidia x 85. 24. Antheridia x 85.

50. Cephalozia (Prionolobus) dentata, (Raddi.)

Hab.—Galton Mountains, British Columbia. (*Lyall.*)

51. Hygrobiella laxifolia, (Hook.) Spruce. Var clavuligera,

Hab.—Greenland: near Lichenfels (Breutel et Curie in Hb. Flot., *Vahl. Syn. Hep.* p. 147.)

52. Pleuroclada albescens, (Hook.) Spruce.

Hab.—Greenland. (*Vahl. Syn. Hep.* p. 102.)

53. Pleuroclada islandica, (Nees.)

Hab.—Greenland. (*Vahl. Syn. Hep.* p. 681.)

54. Anthelia julacea, (Lighf.) Dum.

Hab.—Greenland. (*Vahl. Syn. Hep.* p. 147.)

55. Blepharostoma trichophyllum, (L.) Dum.

Hab.—On earth, Mount Albert, Gaspé, 4,000 ft., 26th August, 1882 (21). On earth, Ste. Anne's River, Gaspé, 17th August, 1882 (17). On old logs, Gaspé Coast, 2nd August, 1882 (16). On rotten wood, British Columbia, 1875 (204). On earth and dead wood, in the Rocky Mountains,

29th July, 1885. On rocks, at Ottawa, 10th October, 1884 (68). (*Macoun.*) Cascade Mountains. (*Lyall.*) Miquelon Island. (*Delàmare.*)

56. **Chandonanthus** setiformis, (Ehrb.) Mitt.

Hab.—Observatory Inlet, N. W. Coast of America. (*Dr. Scouler in Herb. Torrey.*) Mount Albert, Gaspé, 26th August, 1882 (47). (*Macoun.*) Greenland. (*Vahl. in Hb. Hornem.; et G. et Syn. Hep.* p. 130.) Alaska. (*Krause.*)

57. **Kantia** trichomanis, (L.) Gray.

Hab.—On earth or logs, Gaspé Coast, 2nd August, 1882 (24, 49). On earth in woods, Lake Nipissing, 29th May, 1884 (23). On rotten wood, Carlton Place, near Ottawa, 30th May, 1884 (22). On rotten logs, British Columbia (41). (*Macoun.*) Miquelon Island. (*Delàmare.*)

58. **Geocalyx** graveolens, (Schrad.) Nees.

Hab.—On old logs, Belleville, 1875 (220). British Columbia, 1875 (254). On earth, along the Gaspé Coast, 2nd August, 1882 (51). Pirate's Cove, Nova Scotia, 1883 (113). On earth, at Truro, Nova Scotia (175). Jupiter River, Anticosti, 1883 (114). On rotten wood, Red Rock, Lake Superior, 24th June, 1884 (62). On rotten logs, Ottawa, October, 1884 (60, 184). On rotten wood, Vancouver Island, 20th May, 1887 (10). (*Macoun.*) Miquelon Island. (*Delàmare.*)

59. **Scapania Oakesii,** Aust. Bull. Torrey Bot. Club, 3, 10, p. 187.

Hab.—Observatory Inlet, N. W. Coast of America. (*Douglas.*)

60. **Scapania Bolanderi.** Aust. Proc. Phil. Acad. 1869, p. 218.
Scapania caudata Tayl. MS., Scapania albescens Steph., Botanische Jahrb., vol. 8, part 2, p 96, (1886.)

Hab.—On rocks, Lake Superior, 1869 (pp. 213, 214). Vancouver Island, 1875 (27, 28). On stones in brooks, Ottawa, 1883 (231, 249). On rocks, at Truro, Nova Scotia (177). On earth and stones, Pirate's Cove, Nova Scotia, 1883 (100). On moss in woods, Sudbury Junction, 28th May, 1884 (90). (*Macoun.*) Vancouver Island, 1885. (*Dawson.*) On rotten wood (pp. 145, 165, 166). Comox and Nanaimo, V. I., 4th May, 1887 (14, 25, 31, 43, 68, 84, 87). Mount Mark, V.I., 3,000 ft., 26th July, 1887 (100). (*Macoun.*)

N. W. Coast of America. (*Scouler* in *Herb. Taylor.*) Sitcha, American border, (*Mertens in Herb. Lindb.*)   On earth, Vancouver Island. (*Douglas.*)   Alaska. (*Krause.*)

Description of Pl. VII.—Figs. 1-3. Leaves x 16.   4, 5. Postical lobes of leaves x 16.   6. Margin of leaf x 64.   7, 8. Bracts x 16.   9. Perianth x 16.   10. Portion of mouth of perianth x 64 (all 165).

61. Scapania irrigua, Nees.

Hab.—On stones in brooks, 1869 (215a).   In sandy hollows on rocks above Michipicoton, 27th July, 1869 (15a).   Amongst mosses, Peace River, October, 1872 (194a).   British Columbia, 1875 (265). Truro, Nova Scotia (103).   (*Macoun.*)

62. Scapania compacta, (Roth.) Var. grandis,

Hab.—Greenland (Curie et Breutel in Hb. Flotov.) (*Syn. Hep.* p. 64.)

63. Scapania nemorosa, (L.)

Hab.—On rocks, Mount Arrowsmith, Vancouver Island, 17th June, 1887 (94). (*Macoun.*)   British Columbia. (*Lyall.*) Miquelon Island. (*Delàmare.*)   Alaska. (*Krause.*)

64. Scapania undulata, (L.)

Hab.—Observatory Inlet. (*Herb. Torrey.*)   On stones in brooks, 1869 (215).   On boggy ground near a glacier, Selkirk Mountains, August 24th, 1885 (167).   Mount Arrowsmith, Vancouver Island, 5,000 ft., 17th July, 1887 (93), (*Macoun.*) Rocky Mountains. (*Lyall.*) Miquelon Island.   (*Delàmare.*)

65. Scapania uliginosa, Nees.

Hab.—Mount Arrowsmith, Vancouver Island, 4,800 ft., 17th July, 1887 (104).   (*Macoun.*)   Herjedalen (*Hb. Hartm.*)   Greenland. (*Syn. Hep.* p. 67.)

66. Scapania curta, (Mart.)

Hab.—On slate rocks, 10 miles south of Fort William (15).   On earth, Little Slave Lake, Sept. 1872 (241).   On earth, along Ste. Anne's River, Gaspé, 19th August, 1882 (36).   On earth, Anticosti, 1883 (102).   On old logs, Sudbury Junction, 28th May, 1884 (92).   On old logs, Ottawa, 1884 (86, 93).   On rocks, Nipigon River, 1884 (85, 89).   (*Macoun.*)   Unalaschka cl. Chamisso (Hb. Hornschuch.)   (*Syn. Hep.* p. 71.)

67. **Scapania brevicaulis,** Tayl.

Hab.—North America. (*Drummond in Hb. Hook.*)

68. **Scapania glaucocephala,** (Tayl.)

Hab.—On old logs, Belleville, (1867 (265). Peace River, Rocky Mountains, 1872 (206 pp.). On rotten wood, west of the Fraser, British Columbia, 1875 (190). On earth, along the Fraser River, June, 1875 (203). On rotten wood, Porcupine Mountain, Manitoba, 1881 (106). Manitoba Lake, Man., 1881 (105). On logs, Belleville, 1882 (230). On dead wood, Gaspé Coast, August, 1882 (54). On old logs, Mount Albert, Gaspé. 4,000 ft., August, 1882 (34). Ottawa, 1883 (248). On old elm logs, Ottawa, 1883 (229). Ottawa, 1884 (91). (*Macoun.*)

Description of Pl. VIII.—Fig. 1. Plants nat. size. 2. Stem x 24. Origin (Original spec. *Herb. Taylor*). 3-5. Leaves x 24 (106). 6. Upper leaves x 24 (248). 7. Bract x 24 (248). 8. Perianth with bracts x 24 (190). 9. Perianth x 24 (106).

69. **Scapania convexa,** (Scop.)

Jungermania umbrosa, Schrad.

Hab.—On rotten wood, Mount Mark, Vancouver Island, 3,000 ft., 25th July, 1887, ♂ and ♀ *cum per.* (101). (*Macoun.*) Miquelon Island. (*Delàmare.*)

Scapania subalpina, Ness. In a large tuft on rocks 20 miles north of Michipicotin, 27th July, 1869 (34). (*Macoun.*) [Named thus by Austin, but appears to be a form between *S. nemorosa* and *S. undulata.*]

70. **Diplophyllum albicans,** (L.) Dum.

Hab.—On earth, Pictou, Nova Scotia, 1883 (97a). On rocks, Mount Benson, Vancouver Island, 8th June, 1887 (91). On rocks, Mount Arrowsmith, V.1, 17th July, 1887 (96). (*Macoun.*) Rocky Mountains. (*Bourgeau.*) Fort Colville. (*Lyall.*) Miquelon Island. (*Delàmare.*)

Obs.—This species, about the commonest in Europe, appears to be rare in America, as all the specimens that I have seen, except these recorded refer to *Diplophyllum taxifolium.* It is at once recognized by the presence in the two lobes of a pseudo-nerve, which is often colorless, and consists of a series of from 4 to 6 elongated cells, a cross-section of the leaf shows the cells to be of equal diameter as the others, only with the outer walls thickened considerably.

Description of Pl. IX.—Fig. 1. Stem x 24 (97a). 2. Cross-section of leaf x 85 (*France, Du Buysson*). 3. Bract x 24 (*France, Du Buysson*). 4. Perianth x 24 (*France, Du Buysson*).

71. Diplophyllum taxifolium, (Wahlenb.)

Hab.—On rocks, Ste. Anne's River, Gaspé, 20th August, 1882 (88). On moss, Pirate's Cove, Strait of Canso, 1883 (99). (*Macoun.*) On rotten logs, Vancouver Island, 1885. (*Dawson.*) On rocks, Nanaimo River, V.I., 26th April, 1887 (60). (*Macoun.*)

Insula Unalaschka. Hb. L. (*Syn. Hep.* p. 76).

Obs.—This has been usually considered as a variety of the previous species, but Prof. Lindberg regards it as quite distinct, with which opinion I agree; its neater habit, the direction of the postical lobe being more horizontal than in *Diplophyllum albicans*, and the absence of the false nerve, although traces of elongated cells near to the base are sometimes observable, sustain this view.

Description of Pl. IX.—Fig. 5. Fertile stem x 24 (88). 6 Bracts x 24 (88). 7. Perianth with bract x 24 (88).

72. Diplophyllum minutum, (Crantz.)

Hab.—On rocks, near Lake Superior, July, 1869 (197). On rocks, near Lake Nipigon, 10th July, 1884 (79). On rocks, Kicking Horse Lake, Rocky Mountains, 21st July, 1885 (154). (*Macoun.*) Greenland. (*Vahl. Syn. Hep.* p. 679). Alaska. (*Krause.*)

73. Diplophyllum argenteum, (Tayl. hb.) Spruce.

"Folia transversa, superiora equitantia, ad ¾ complicato-biloba, lobis lanceolatis acuminatis, antico postico subæquilongo sæpius duplo angustiore, margine grosse serrata, basi crenulata. Bractæ 3-jugæ, confertissimæ, intimæ suborbiculatæ ad ½ 2-4-lobæ lacinulato-spinulosæ. Per. emersum ovali-fusiforme, ab ipsa basi obtuse 12-plicatum, ore in cilia numerosissima flexuosa intexta fissum, quasi-tomentosum." (*Spruce Hep. Amaz. et And* page 417.)

Hab.—On rotten wood, Vancouver Island, 1885 (162). (*Dawson.*) N. W. coast of America. (*Dr. Scouler in Herb. Taylor.*) Observatory Inlet, (*Dr. Scouler in Herb. Torrey.*) N. W. coast of America. (*Menzies, 1791 in Herb. R. Spruce.*)

74. Jungermania polita, Nees.

Hab.—On earth, along the coast, Gaspé, 21st July, 1882 (170 pp.). (*Macoun.*)

75. **Jungermania Crœnlandica,** Nees.

Greenland (Breutel et Curie in **Hb.** Flotoviano N. 2). (*Syn. Hep.* p. 114.)

76. **Jungermania Kunzeana,** Huben.

Hab.—Amongst mosses, Peace River, 1872 (194). On rotten wood, British Columbia, 1875, ♂ and ♀ *cum per.* (189). On rocks, Lake Nipigon, 17th July, 1884 (77). Peat bogs, Nipigon River, 3rd July, 1884 (73, 78). (*Macoun.*)

77. **Jungermania Michauxii,** Web.

Hab.—On rocks, west of Lake Superior, 1872 (200). On logs, Ste. Anne's River, Gaspé, *cum per.*, 19th August, 1882 (33). On rotten logs and rocks, Nova Scotia, 1883 (98), On the perpendicular face of rocks, Lake Nipigon, Ontario, 4th July, 1884 (63). (*Macoun.*) Canada. (*Syn. Hep.* p. 120). Near Fort Colville, and Columbia River. (*Lyall.*)

78. **Jungermania saxicola,** Schrad.

Hab.—On earth in bogs, Mount Albert, Gaspé, 26th August, 1882 (47). (*Macoun.*) Greenland. (*Vahl. Syn. Hep.* p. 119). Alaska. (*Krause.*)

79. **Jungermania Helleriana,** Nees.

Hab.—Near Lake Superior, 1869 (217). On logs, Vancouver Island, 1875 (210). (*Macoun.*)

80. **Lophocolea bidentata, (L.)** Dum.

Hab.—Vancouver Island, 6th May, 1875 (33). On dead wood, Comox, V.I., 27th July, 1887 (75). (*Macoun.*)

81. **Lophocolea heterophylla,** (Schrad.)

Hab.—On rotten wood, Ottawa, 1884 (130). On rotten logs, Nipigon River, 6th July, 1884. (*Macoun.*) Canada. (*Hb. Austin.*) Fort Colville. (*Lyall.*) "The few fragments supposed to belong to this species in Lyall's collection are merely sufficient to indicate the presence of something very nearly allied if not identical." (*Mitt.*) Miquelon Island. (*Delamare.*)

82. **Lophocolea minor,** Nees.

Hab.—On rocks, Belleville, 1867 (201). British Columbia, 1875

2

(240). Ottawa, 1883 (243). On rocks, near Ottawa, 1884 (29). (*Macoun.*)

Description of Pl. X.—Fig. 1. Plants nat. size. 2. Stems x 24 (29). 3, 4. Leaves x 24 (124). 5. Leaf x 24 (201). 6, 7. Branch leaves x 24 (201). 8. Underleaf x 85 (240). 9-11. Underleaves from upper part of stem x 85 (29). 12, 13. Bracts x 24 (240). 14, 15. Bracts x 24 (201). 16. Bracteole x 85 (240). 17. Bracteole x 24 (240). 18. Bracteole x 24 (201). 19. Pistillidium x 85 (201).

83. Lophocolea Macounii, Aust. Proc. Ac. Nat. Sc. Philad. p. 223, 1869.

Hab.—On rotten wood, Ottawa, 1883 (247). On rotten logs, Nipigon River, Ontario, July 6, 1884 (61). (*Macoun.*)

84. Harpanthus scutatus, (Web. et Mohr.) Nees.

Hab.—Pirate's Cove, Nova Scotia (119 pp.). On rotten wood, at Belleville, 1865 (202). On old logs, at Belleville, 1867 (199). On rotten wood, near Belleville, October, 1870, *cum per.* On rotten wood, Lake Nipissing, Ontario, ♂ et ♀ *cum per.*, 28th May, 1884 (66). On rotten wood, Nipigon River, 6th July, 1884 (71). On earth and mosses, 21st July, 1885 (150). (*Macoun.*) Miquelon Island. (*Delamare,*)

85. Harpanthus Flotowii, Nees.

Hab.—Greenland. (*Syn. Hep.* p. 170.) Rocky Mountains. (*Bourgeau.*)

86. Chiloscyphus polyanthus, (L.) Corda.

Hab.—On logs, at Truro, Nova Scotia, 13th June, 1883 (173). On dead wood, Comox, V.I., 29th April, 1887 (56, 70). On rocks in streams, Nanaimo, V.I., 3rd June, 1887 (79). (*Macoun.*) Near Fort Colville. (*Lyall.*) Miquelon Island. (*Delamare.*)

87. Chiloscyphus adscendens, Hook. and Wils.

Hab.—On rotten wood, Belleville, 1868 (207). (*Macoun.*) West of the Fraser River, B.C., June, 1875. (*Hb. Austin.*) Vancouver Island, 3rd May, 1887 (41a). (*Macoun.*)

88. Mylia Taylori, (Hook.) Gray.

Hab.—On logs subject to inundation, Ste. Anne's River, Gaspé, 16th August, 1882 (58). On logs and in swamps, Mount Albert, Gaspé, 26th August, 1882 (44), with perianths. On the summit of

Mount Albert, Gaspé, 27th August, 1882 (83). On dead wood and in wet places, Pirate's Cove, Nova Scotia, 1883 (108, 109, 115). (*Macoun.*) Greenland. (*Vahl. Syn. Hep.* p. 668.) Newfoundland. (*Syn. Hep.* p. 82.) (*Du Preaux in Hb. Moug.*) Cascade Mountains. (*Lyall.*) Miquelon Island. (*Delamare.*)

89. Mylia anomala, (Hook.)

Hab.—Peace River, Rocky Mountains, 1872 (186). Peat bog, Anticosti, 1883 (107), with perianths. (*Macoun.*)

90. Arnellia fennica, (Gray.) Lindb. (*Jung. Fennica*, Gottsch.)
Southyba fennica, Lindb. olim.)

Hab.—On rocks, Lake Manitoba, 1881 (182). On earth and logs, Rocky Mountains,23rd July, 1885 (156). (*Macoun.*)

Obs.—New to America. I add the following interesting note from Dr. Spruce:—"Many thanks for the Canadian specimens of *Southbya fennica*. It is one more link in the chain of facts that prove the essential uniformity of the hepatic flora of the whole North Temperate Zone. My friend, Alfred Wallace, has been on a lecturing tour in America. I did not ask him to gather me any hepatics, but he has sent me two; the one from the Sierra Nevada (abt. 9,000 ft.) is *Jung. ventricosa;* the other, from the Rocky Mountains (alt. 14,000 ft.), is *Jung. barbata.*" Both these are among the commonest European species.

91. Plagiochila porelloides, (Torrey.) Lindenb.

Hab.—Vancouver Island, 1875 (5). Ste. Anne's River, Gaspé, August, 1882 (27, 55, 56, 57). On earth along brooks, Yarmouth, N.S., 25th June, 1883 (169). On stones along brooks, Belleville, 16th June, 1884 (94). On overflowed ground, Sudbury Junction, 28th May, 1884 (95). On rocks, Dog Island, Lake Nipigon, 17th July, 1884 (96). On earth near water, Vancouver Island, April, May, 1887 (28, 34, 48, 51). (*Macoun.*)

Description of Pl. XI.—Fig. 1. Plant nat. size. 2. Branch x 11. 3-6. Leaves x 11. 7. Outer bract x 17. 8, 9. Bracts x 17. 10. Perianth x 11 (all 57).

92. Plagiochila porelloides vár. nodosa, (*Plag. nodosa*, Lindenb.)

Hab.—North America. (*Drummond Hb. Hook.*) Mountain ravines, Canada. (*vide Austin.*)

93. Plagiochila asplenioides, (L.)

Hab.—Fort Colville. (*Lyall. in Herb. Mitt.*)

94. Leptoscyphus interruptus, (Nees.) Mitt.

Hab.—Greenland. (*Vahl. Syn. Hep.* p. 645.)

95. Jungermania cordifolia, Hook.

Hab.—On stones in brooks at Owen Sound, Ont., October, 1874 (188). On stones, Ste. Anne's River, Gaspé, 30th August, 1882 (25), with perianth. (*Macoun.*) Greenland. (*Syn. Hep.* p. 95). Alaska. (*Krause.*)

96. Jungermania cordifolia, var. **Vahliana,**

Hab.—Greenland. (*Vahl. Syn. Hep.* p. 675.) Fort Colville and Galton Mountains. (*Lyall.*)

Jungermania tersa. Nees.

Hab.—Galton Mountains. (*Lyall., fide Mitt.*)

[I believe that this species is to be referred to *Jungermania cordifolia* (*Hook*) or to *Jungermania riparia* (*Taylor*), original specimens from Nees having been found to be both these.]

97. Jungermania riparia, Tayl.

Hab.—On wet earth, Vancouver Island, 3rd May, 1887 (40). On stones in brooks, V. I., 19th May, 1887 (7), with perianths. (*Macoun.*) On stones in the Colville River, Fort Colville. (*Lyall.*)

98. Liochlœna lanceolata, Nees.

Hab.—Mooyie River, British Columbia. (*Lyall. in Herb. Mitt.*) Miquelon Island. (*Delamare.*)

99. Cymnocolea inflata, (Huds.) Dum.

Hab.—On rocks, Lake Superior, 1869 (192). On boggy ground, Mount Albert, Gaspé, 26th August, 1882 (52a). (*Macoun.*) Greenland. (*Vahl. Syn. Hep.* p. 677.) Miquelon Island. (*Delamare.*)

100. Jungermania autumnalis, De C. (*Jungermania Schraderi,* Mart.) (*Jungermania subapicalis,* Nees.)

Hab.—Lake Superior, 1869. On rotten wood, Ottawa, 1884 (185), *cum per.* On wet earth, Vancouver Island, 3rd May, 1887 (40a).

(*Macoun.*) **Vars.** α and β Greenland. (*Vahl.* **Syn.**) (*Hep.* p. 668.) About Fort Colville and the Colville River. (*Lyall.* in Herb. *Mitt.*) **Miquelon Island** (*Delamare*) as *Jungermania subapicalis*, Nees, and **new** for America. Austin (Bull. Torr. Bot., vol. VI., 16th April, 1876) gives *Jungermania subapicalis* as synonym for *Jungermania Schraderi* (*Mart.*).

101. Jungermania exsecta, Schmid.

Hab.—On rotten wood, British Columbia, 1875 (208a). On rocks, Anticosti (101). On rocks and earth at Morley, June, 1885. (159a). (*Macoun.*) North America. (*Drummond.*) Fort Colville. (*Lyall,* fide *Mitt.*)

Obs.—This is a somewhat variable species, the commonest form in Canada being that described by Dr. Taylor as *Jung. scitula*; it is larger, less gemmiparous, with leaves more frequently tridentate than in the common European form.

Hab.—New Brunswick, Canada. (*James*, in Herb. *Aust.*) On earth, Lake Superior, 1869 (213). On earth and logs, Coast of Gaspé, August, 1882 (48). On rotten logs, Belleville. Ottawa, 1883 (227, 260, 233), On rotten logs, Ottawa, October, 1884 (87). On rotten logs, British Columbia, 1885 (239). (*Macoun.*)

Description of Pl. XII.—Fig. 1. Portion of stem. (*Hook. Brit. Jung.,* Tab. XIX., Fig. 4). 2, 3, 4. Leaves x 24 (48). 5-9. Leaves x 24 (*Baden, Jack.*). 10-11. Bracts x 24 (239). 12. Perianth x. 24. 13-14. Perigonial leaves x 24 (*Baden, Jack.*). 15. Antheridium x 85 (48).

102. Jungermania quinquedentata, Web. (J. Lyoni. Tayl.)

Hab.—On earth, Lake Superior, *cum per.* 1869 (216). On old logs, Manitoba, 1881 (180). On logs, Gaspé coast, 2nd August, 1882 (50). On moss, Sudbury Junction, 28th May, 1884. On rocks, Lake Nipigon, 10th July, 1884 (65). On rocks, Dog Island, Lake Nipigon, 17th July, 1884 (74). On logs, Rocky Mountains, August, 1885 (160). (*Macoun.*) Galton Mountains. (*Lyall* vide *Mitt.*)

103. Jungermania lycopodioides, Wallr.

Hab.—On logs in woods, British Columbia, 1872 (196). On rocks, Lake Winnipegoosis, 27th June, 1881 (41). On rocks, at Campbellton, New Brunswick, 2nd September, 1882 (42). Stupart's Bay, Hudson Strait, 1884 (108). On rocks, Selkirk Mountains, 21st July, 1885 (157). On boggy ground, Selkirk Mountains, July 23rd, 1885 (163). (*Macoun.*) Greenland. (*Vahl.*) (*Syn. Hep.* p. 125.) Galton Mountains, and on stones in the Columbia River. (*Lyall,* vide *Mitt.*)

104. Jungermania Flœrkii, Web. et Mohr.

Hab.—On rocks, commou, Rocky Mountains, 29th July, 1885 (159). On rocks and earth, Morley, 14th June, 1885 (158). On earth, Nanaimo, Vancouver Island, 4th June, 1887 (89). On rocks, Mount Mark, Vancouver Island, 3,000 feet, 27th July, 1887 (76). (*Macoun.*) Kettle Falls, Columbia River. (*Lyall* vide *Mitt.*)

105. Jungermania Flœrkii, var. **alpina.**

Hab.—On earth, Rocky Mountains, 7,000 feet, 20th July, 1885 (155). (*Macoun.*)

Obs.—In this form the basal postical teeth entirely disappear, or only a single tooth is apparent; the underleaves are bifid with one or rarely, two teeth at each side of the base; its nearest ally is *Jung. Kunzeana Hüben.*

106. Jungermania Flœrkii, var.

Hab.—Greenland. (*Currie.*) (*Syn. Hep.* 124.)

107. Jungermania barbata, Schreb.

Hab.—Lake Superior, 1872 (262). British Columbia, 1875 (225). On rocks, Lake Nipigon, 10th July, 1884 (76). On rocks in the Rocky Mountains, 29th July, 1885 (143, 159). On rotten logs, Lake Nipissing, 28th May, 1884 (67). (*Macoun.*) Greenland. (*Vahl.*) (*Syn. Hep.* p. 680.) Miquelon Island. (*Delàmare.*)

108. Jungermania attenuata, Lindenb.

Hab.—Along Lake Superior, 1869 (261). Ottawa, 1883 (232). On earth, Pictou, Nova Scotia, 1883 (97). Summit of Mount Albert, Gaspé, 4,000 feet, 26th August, 1882 (40). (*Macoun.*)

109. Jungermania incisa, Schrad.

Hab.—Peace River, 1872 (187), *cum per.* On rotten wood, British Columbia, 1875 (191). On logs, Ste. Anne's River, Gaspé, 16th August, 1882 (45). Truro, Nova Scotia, 1883 (124). Jupiter River, Anticosti, 1883 (120a, 126). Ottawa, 1884 (178, 237). On rotten wood, Nipigon Lake, 26th June, 1884 (75). On logs, Rocky Mountains, 24th August, 1885 (160). On rotten wood, Comox, V.I., 30th April, 1887 (32, 49). (*Macoun.*) Fort Colville. (*Lyall* vide *Mitt.*) Miquelon Island. (*Delàmare.*)

110. **Jungermania Wattiana,** Aust.   Bull. Torrey Bot. Club,
3, 2, 187.

Hab.—Near Lake Superior, 1869.   **Peace River,** 1872.   (*Hb. Aust.*)
(*Macoun.*)

111. **Jungermania capitata,** Hook.

Hab.—On rotten wood, British Columbia, 1875 (238), *cum per.*   On
rotten wood, Selkirk Mountains, B.C., 21st August, 1881 (161).
(*Macoun.*)

112. **Jungermania bicrenata,** Lindenb.

Hab.—On earth, Lake Nipissing, 29th May, 1884 (82).   (*Macoun.*)

113. **Jungermania alpestris,** Schleich.

Hab.—On stones in brooks, **Lake Superior,** 1869 (215).   On earth,
Mount Mark, Vancouver Island, 26th July, 1887 (107).   (*Macoun.*)

114. **Jungermania ventricosa,** Dicks.

Hab.—On House Mountain, Little Slave Lake, 1872 (193).   On
moss and earth, Rocky Mountains, 1872 (206).   On earth along the
Gaspé Coast, 2nd August, 1882 (39).   On logs, Coast of Gaspé, 8th
August, 1882 (37).   On earth in woods, Ste. Anne's River, Gaspé,
20th August, 1882 (27a).   Jupiter River, Anticosti, 1883 (120.)
On rocks, Lake Nepigon, 10th July, 1884 (64).   Vancouver Island and
Fort Colville.   (*Lyall* vide *Mitt.*)   Alaska.   (*Krause.*)

115. **Jungermania ventricosa,** Dicks. var. **porphyroleuca,**
Nees.

Hab.—On rotten logs, Victoria, Vancouver Island, 1875, *cum per,*
(211, 212).   On old logs, Gaspé Coast, 2nd August, 1882 (26).   On
rocks, Lake Nipissing, 10th July, 1884 (65a).   On rotten wood,
Columbia Valley, 7th July, 1885 (148).   On earth and rocks, Rocky
Mountains, 21st July, 1885 (149).   Vancouver Island, 1887 (35).
(*Macoun*).

116. **Jungermania ventricosa,** Dicks. var. **longiflora,** Nees.?

Hab.—On logs in woods, Gaspé, 8th August, 1882 (28).   (*Macoun.*)

117. **Jungermania ventricosa,** Dicks. var.

Hab.—On rocks, Vancouver Island, 9th May, 1887 (24).   (*Macoun.*)

118. **Jungermania Mülleri,** Nees.

Hab.—On earth, along the Gaspé Coast, 21st Aug., 1882 (170 pp.). (*Macoun.*) Miquelon Island. (*Delàmare.*)

119. **Jungermania Mülleri,** Nees. var. **maritima.**

Hab.—File Hills, near Qu'Appelle, July, 1879 (116). On earth, along the Gaspé Coast, 8th August, 1882 (53). (*Macoun.*)

120. **Jungermania Vahliana,** Nees.

"Caule radiculoso, inter muscos repente, stolonifero apice adscendente; foliis confertis, flavo-fuscis, ovato-quadratis, erecto-patulis subcomplicatisque v. patenti-deflexis subsquarrosis ad medium usque bilobis v. rarius trilobis, lobis ovatis obtusis (spermatocystidiis interdum apice subhirtis et irregulariter dentatis), prope basin dorsalem subdecurrentem dente v. lobulo dentiformi ornatis; amphigastriis majoribus versiformibus, aliis simplicioribus indivisis, ovato-lanceolatis, utirnque basin versus dente lineari acutis (in gemmis), aliis bifidis, profunde bipartitis, lobis lanceolato-acuminatis, basi uno alterove dente armatis (in caulibus); fructificatio ignota. Gottsche in litt.; N. v. Es. in mscr. Specimina depicta in sinu Baals Revier Groenlandiæ leg. beat. Dr. J. Vahl."—Lindberg, S. O. *Revisio critica iconum in opere Flora Danica muscos illustrantium* (Acta Societ. Fennicae, X, Helsingfors 1871). "Revue Bryologique" n. 6 p. 105, 1883.

121. **Jungermania anacampta,** Tayl. (*Jung. Michauxii,* fide *Mitt.*)

Hab.—North America. (*Drummond, Hb. Hook.*)

122. **Jungermania colpodes,** Tayl.

Hab.—North America. (*Drummond, Hb. Hook.*)

123. **Jungermania crenulata,** Sm.

Hab.—Ottawa, 1883 (253). Truro, Nova Scotia, 1883 (110, 127). (*Macoun.*) Greenland. (*Vahl.*) (*Syn. Hep.* p. 674.)

124. **Nardia compressa,** (Hook.) Gray.

Hab.—Greenland. (*Vahl.*) (*Syn. Hep.* p. 12.)

125. **Nardia scalaris,** (Schrad.)

Hab.—On earth, Nanaimo, Vancouver Island, 6th June, 1887 (83). (*Macoun.*)

Obs.—First record for America of this somewhat common European species.

126. **Marsupella emarginata,** (Ehrh). Dum

Hab.—Mount Benson, Vancouver Island, 3000 feet altitude, 8th June, 1887 (46). Mount Mark, Vancouver Island, 3000 feet altitude, 26th July, 1887 (106). (*Macoun.*) Miquelon Island. (*Delàmare.*)

127. **Marsupella emarginata,** (Ehrh.) var.

Hab.—Mount Benson, Vancouver Island, 8th June, 1887 (90). On earth, Nanaimo, Vancouver Island, 4th June, 1887 (88). (*Macoun.*)

128.—**Marsupella emarginata,** Var. **aquatica.**

Hab.—Newfoundland. (*In II b. M.* sub. 219. *Syn. Hep.* p. 7.)

129.—**Marsupella sphacelata,** (Giesecke.)

Hab.—On rocks, Yarmouth, Nova Scotia, 1883 (121). (*Macoun.*) Greenland. (*Vahl.*) (*Syn. Hep.* p. 7.) Alaska. (*Krause.*) Miquelon Island. (*Delàmare.*)

130.—**Marsupella sparsifolia,** (Lindb.)

Hab.—On wet rocks, Nanaimo, Vancouver Island, (78). Mount Arrowsmith, Vancouver Island, 4800 feet altitude (103). (*Macoun.*)

Obs.—First record for America.

131. **Cesia corallioides,** (Nees.) Gray.

Hab.—Alaska. (*Krause.*)

132. **Cesia obtusa,** Lindb.

Hab.—Near Frederickshaab, Greenland. (*Vahl.*)

133. **Cesia concinnata,** (Dicks.)

Hab.—Mount Benson, Vancouver Island, 3rd June, 1887 (45). Mount Mark, Vancouver Island, 3,000 ft. altitude (92). (*Macoun.*) Alaska. (*Krause.*)

134. **Fossombronia longiseta,** Aust.

Hab.—On earth, Vancouver Island, 9th May, 1887 (26). (*Macoun.*)

135. **Fossombronia pusilla,** (L.) Radd.?

Hab.—On the roadside, Hastings Co., Ontario, 1870 (223). On earth, Sproat Lake, Vancouver Island, 12th Aug., 1887 (98 and 99).

(*Macoun.*) These specimens are imperfect and destitute of spores ; they all agree in having the strong smell of *pusilla*, to which I doubtfully refer them.

136. Fossombronia Macouni, Aust.

Hab.—Portage la Loche (Methy Portage), lat. 57°, 1875. (*Macoun.*)

137. Blasia pusilla, (L.) Mich.

Hab.—On earth, Gaspé Coast, August, 1882 (1 and 2). (*Macoun.*)

138. Pellia endiviæfolia, (Dick.) Radd.

Hab.—On earth in ditches, Nanaimo, Vancouver Island, 2nd June, 1887 (80). (*Macoun.*)

139. Pellia epiphylla, (J.)

Hab.—Miquelon Island. (*Delamare.*)

140. Aneura latifrons, (Lindb.)

Hab.—Anticosti, 1883 (117.)   On rotten wood, Comox, Vancouver Island, 29th April, 1887 (62, 63 and 64).   On rotten wood, Nanaimo, Vancouver Island, 3rd June, 1887 (81.) (*Macoun.*) Miquelon Island. (*Delamare.*)

141. Aneura sessilis, (Sprengel.) Dum.

Hab.—On moss and earth, Carleton Place, near Ottawa, 30th May, 1884 (6). (*Macoun.*)

142. Aneura pinguis, (L.) Dum.

Hab.—Amongst mosses in peat swamps, Ont., 1874 (222). On moss, St. Mary's River, Anticosti (112).   On sticks in pools, Vancouver Island, 1887 (30). (*Macoun.*)

143. Aneura palmata, (Hedw.)

Hab.—On rotten stumps, at Belleville, 17th Sept., 1874 (221). Ottawa, 1883 (235 and 236). On old logs, Vancouver Island, 20th May, 1887 (9). (*Macoun.*)

144. Aneura multifida, (L.) var. ambrosioides.

Hab.—On earth in pools, Vancouver Island, 3rd May, 1887 (29). (*Macoun.*)

145. **Metzgeria pubescens,** (Schrank.) Radd.

Hab.— On boulders, Rocky Mountains, 5,000 ft. alt., 29th July, 1885 (137). (*Macoun.*) British Columbia. (*Lyall.*) Alaska. (*Krause.*)

146. **Metzgeria myriopoda,** Lindb.

Hab.—On rocks, near Ottawa, 1885 (129). (*Macoun.*)

147. **Metzgeria conjugata,** Lindb.

Hab.—Ottawa, 1883 (244). (*Macoun.*) At the base of trees, Vancouver Island, 1885 (138). (*Dawson.*) On earth, along a river at Comox, V.I., (35, 50). (*Macoun*).

148. **Marchantia polymorpha,** (L.)

Hab.—On earth in swamp, Gaspé, 1882 (3). On earth, Vancouver Island, 29th May, 1887 (1). (*Macoun.*) Saskatchewan and Rocky Mountains. (*Bourgeau.*) Fort Colville and Sinkyakwateen. (*Lyall.*) Alaska. (*Krause.*)

149. **Fimbriaria violacea,** Aust.

Hab.—On wet soil, Selkirk Mountains, 2nd August, 1885 (134). (*Macoun.*)

150. **Fimbriaria pilosa,** (Wahlenb.) Tayl.

Hab.—On the upper slopes of the Rocky Mountains, 21st July, 1885 (133). On earth, at Comox, Vancouver Island, 29th April, 1887 (72); British Columbia. (*Macoun.*) Greenland. (*Vahl.*) (*Syn. Hep.* 558.)

151. **Fimbriaria tenella,** Nees.

Hab.—On earth, Vancouver Island, 9th May, 1887 (23). (*Macoun.*)

(152. **Clevea hyalina,** (Somm. Lindb.

Hab.—On earth, near a glacier, Selkirk Mountains, 5000 feet, 21st Aug., 1885 (135). Rocky Mountains, 7500 feet, 21st July, 1885 (132). (*Macoun.*) Rittenbenk, Greenland (1265). (*J. Vahl.*)

153. **Ricciella fluitans,** (L.) Braun.

Hab.—Marshes, at Belleville, 7th August, 1873 (218). (*Macoun.*)

154. **Ricciella fluitans, var. terrestris.**

On mud at Belleville, 1870 (220), 1871 (219).

155. **Ricciocarpus natans,** (L.) Cord.

Hab.—In a lake, Vancouver Island, 27th May, 1887 (3).   (*Macoun.*) *Canada,* fide *Underwood.*

156. **Riccia lutescens,** (Schwein.)

Hab.—*Canada,* fide *Underwood.*

157. **Anthoceros laevis,** (L.)

Hab.—*Canada,* fide *Underwood.*

158. **Anthoceros punctatus,** (L.)

Hab.—*Canada,* fide *Underwood.* Leamy's Lake, near Ottawa, Ont., 1889. (*Macoun.*)

159. **Anthoceras laciniatus,** (Schwein.)

Hab.—*Canada,* vide *Austin.* (Bull. Torrey Bot., vol. VI., April, 1875.)

160. **Anthoceros fusiformis,** Aust.

Hab.—On earth, Vancouver Island, 1885 (136)   (*Dawson.*)   On damp earth, V.I., 27th May, 1887 (2).   Roadside, Nanaimo, V.I., 9th July, 1887 (97). (*Macoun.*) Observatory Islet. (*Scouler,* vide *Austin.*)

161. **Notothylas orbicularis,** (Schwein.) Sulliv.

Hab.—*Canada,* vide *Underwood.*

162. **Duvalia rupestris,** (Nees.)

Hab.—Calcareous or slaty rocks, Belleville, Ontario. (*Macoun.*)

163. **Reboulia hemisphærica,** (L.) Radd.

Hab.—Canada to Hudson Bay, vide *Underwood.*

164. **Preissia commutata,** Nees.

Hab.—On calcareous earth, Gaspé Coast, 10th Aug., 1882 (4). (*Macoun.*) Alaska. (*Krause.*)

165. **Hepatica conica,** (L.) Mich. **Conocephalus conicus,** Necker.

Hab.—On earth, by brooks near Ottawa, 1884, (5) On earth at Ottawa, 15th May, 1885 (171). (*Macoun.*) British Columbia, near Fort Colville. (*Lyall.*) Alaska. (*Krause.*)

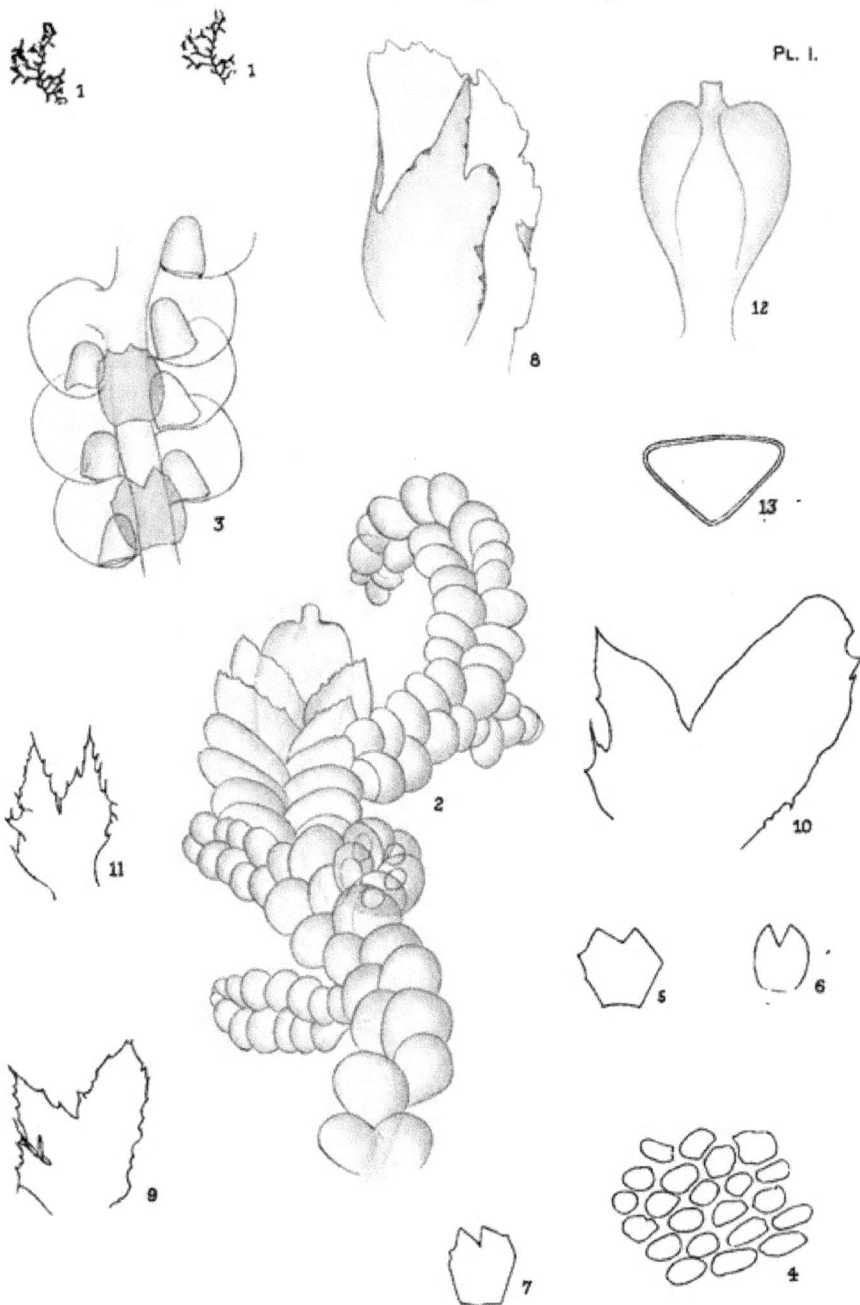

PL. I.

W. H. P, del.

Mortimer & Co. Lith.

Fruilania Selwyniana.

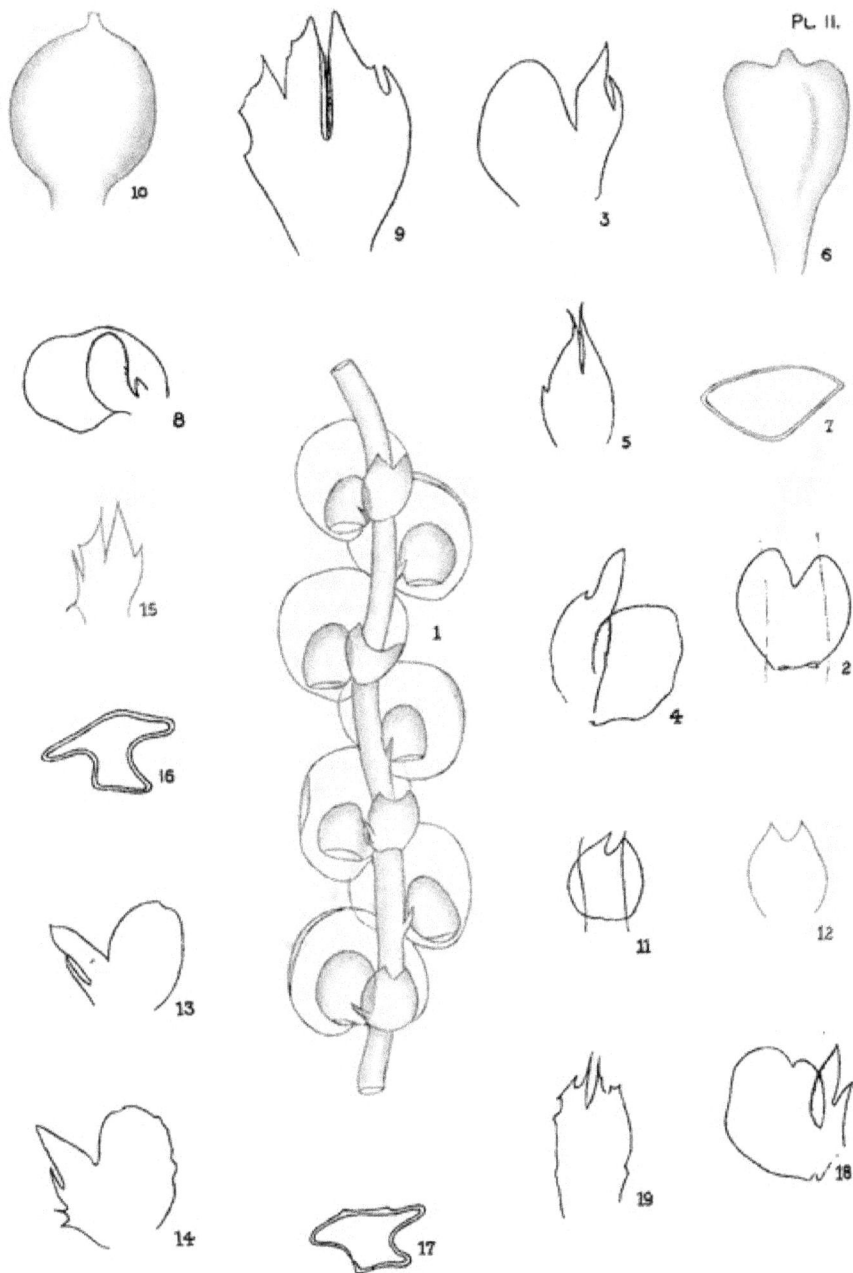

Frullania Eboracensis.

PL. III.

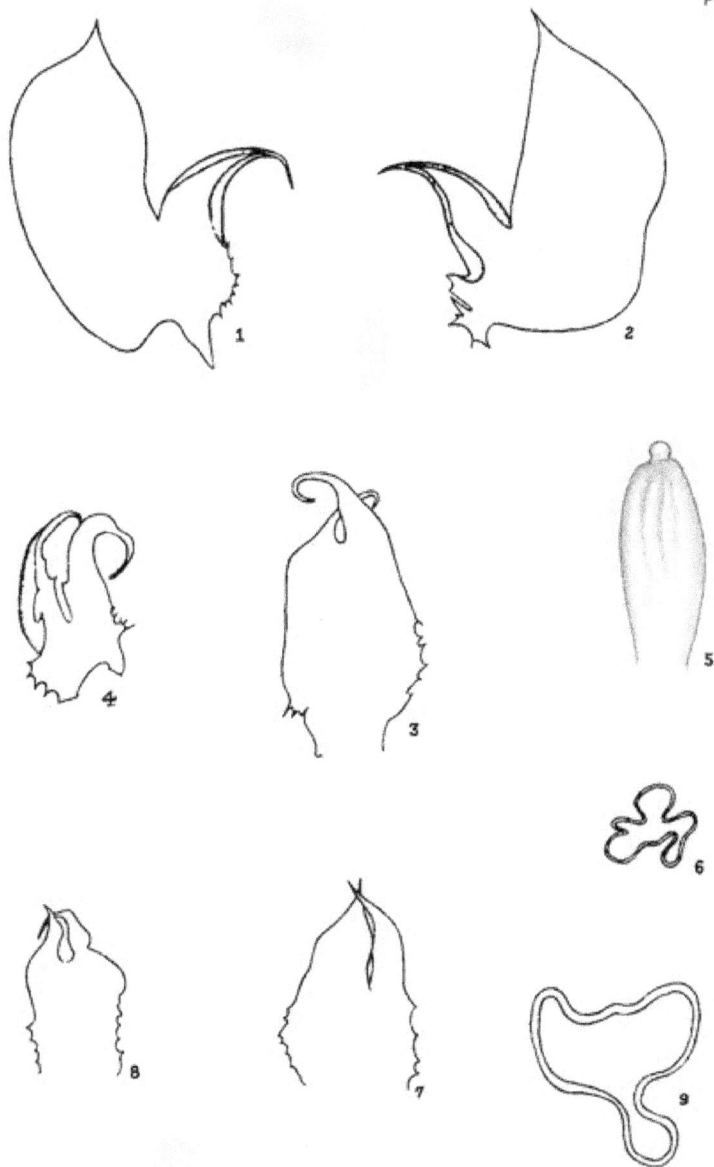

W. H. P. del.

Mortimer & Co. Lith.

Frullania Nisquallensis.

PL. IV.

1

2

4

3

W. H. P. del.

Mortimer & Co. Lith.

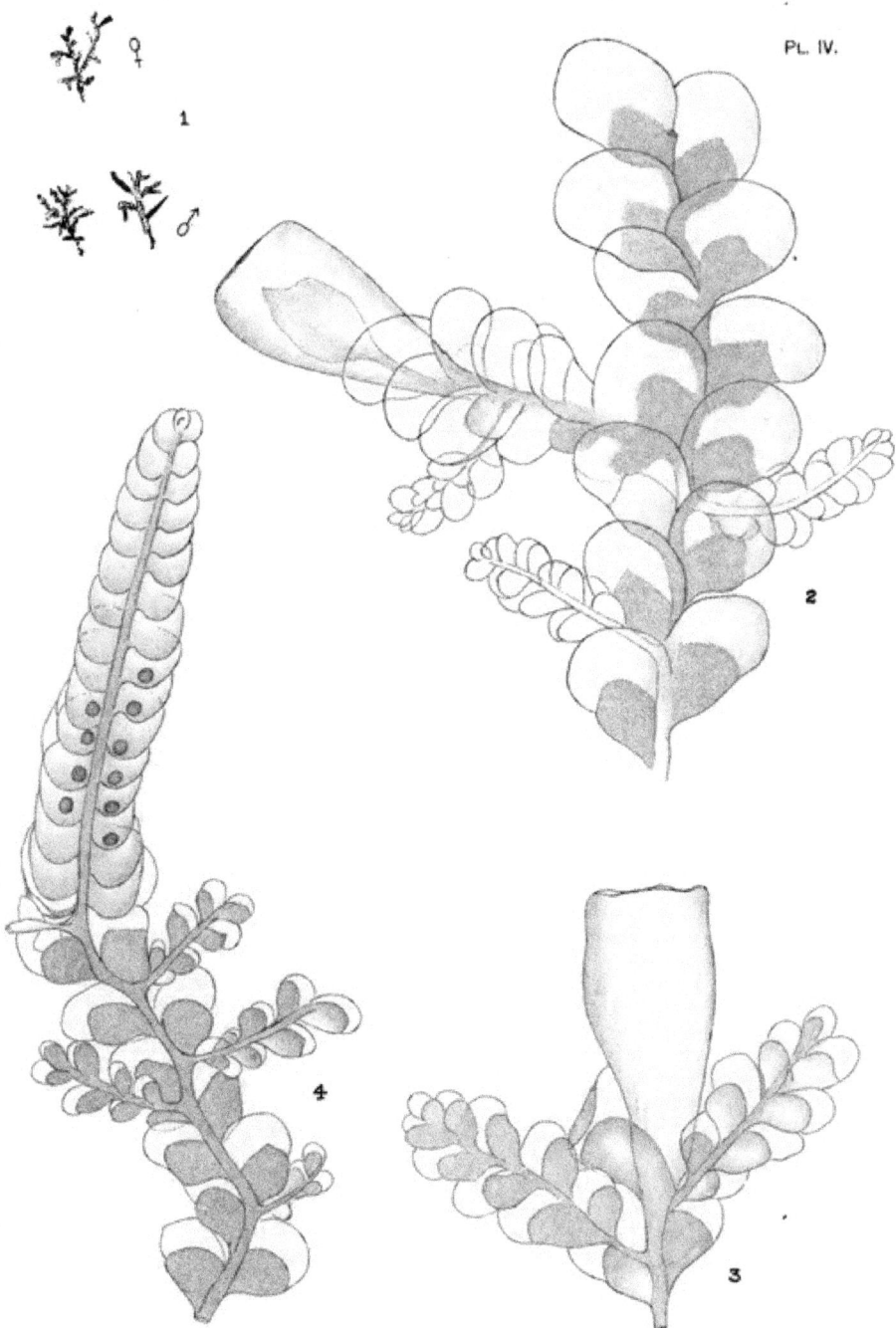

Radula spicata.

Pl. V.

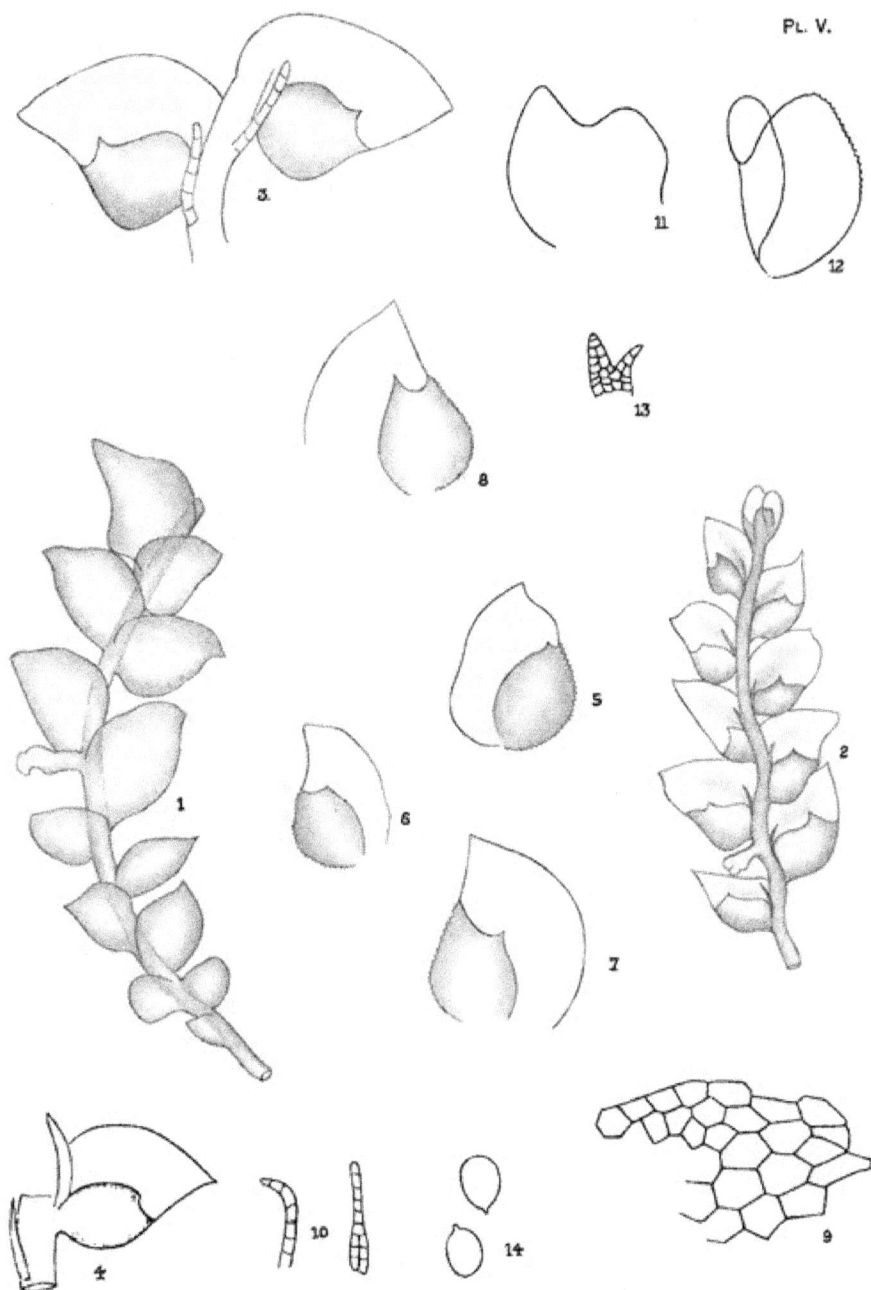

W. H. P, del.

Mortimer & Co. Lith.

Lejeunea Biddlecomiæ

PL. VI.

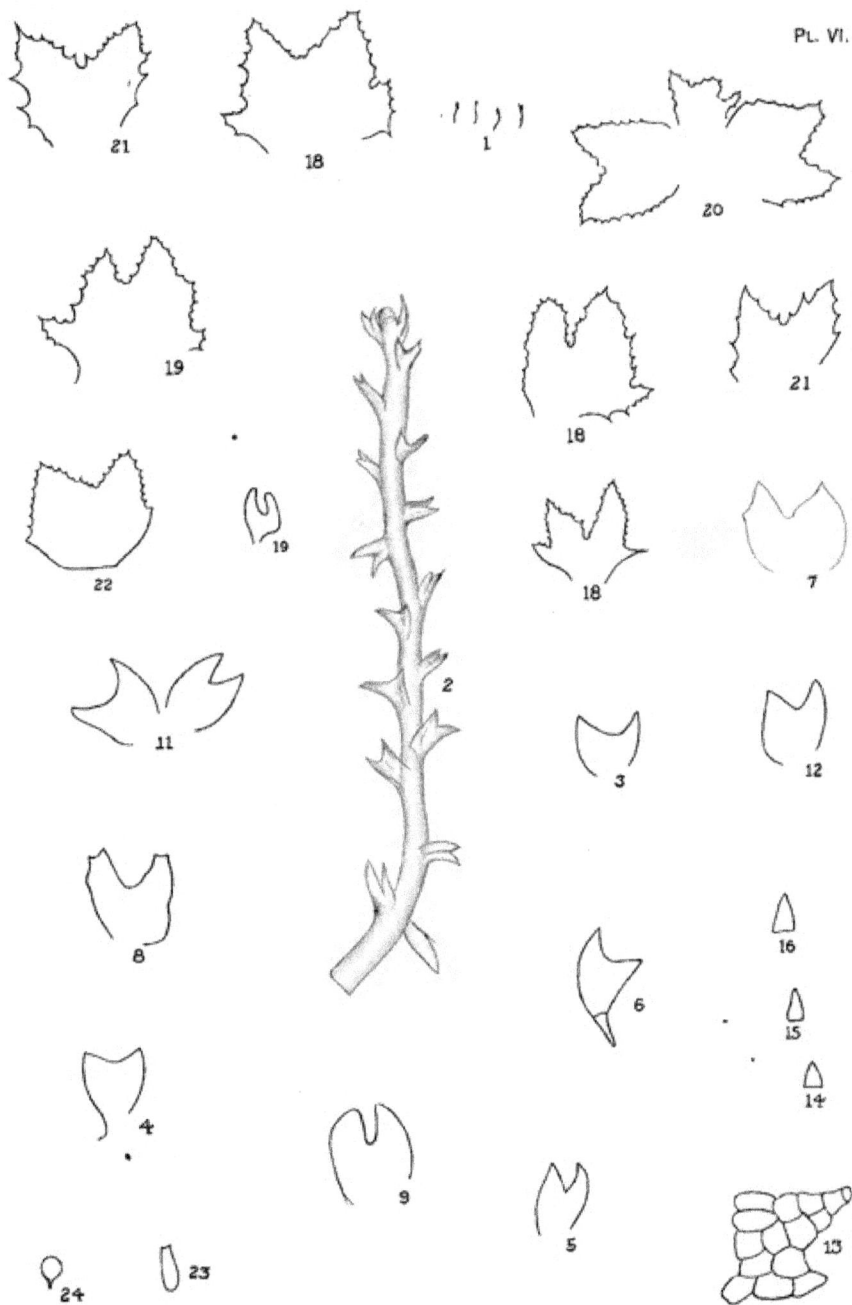

Cephalozia minima.

Pl. VII.

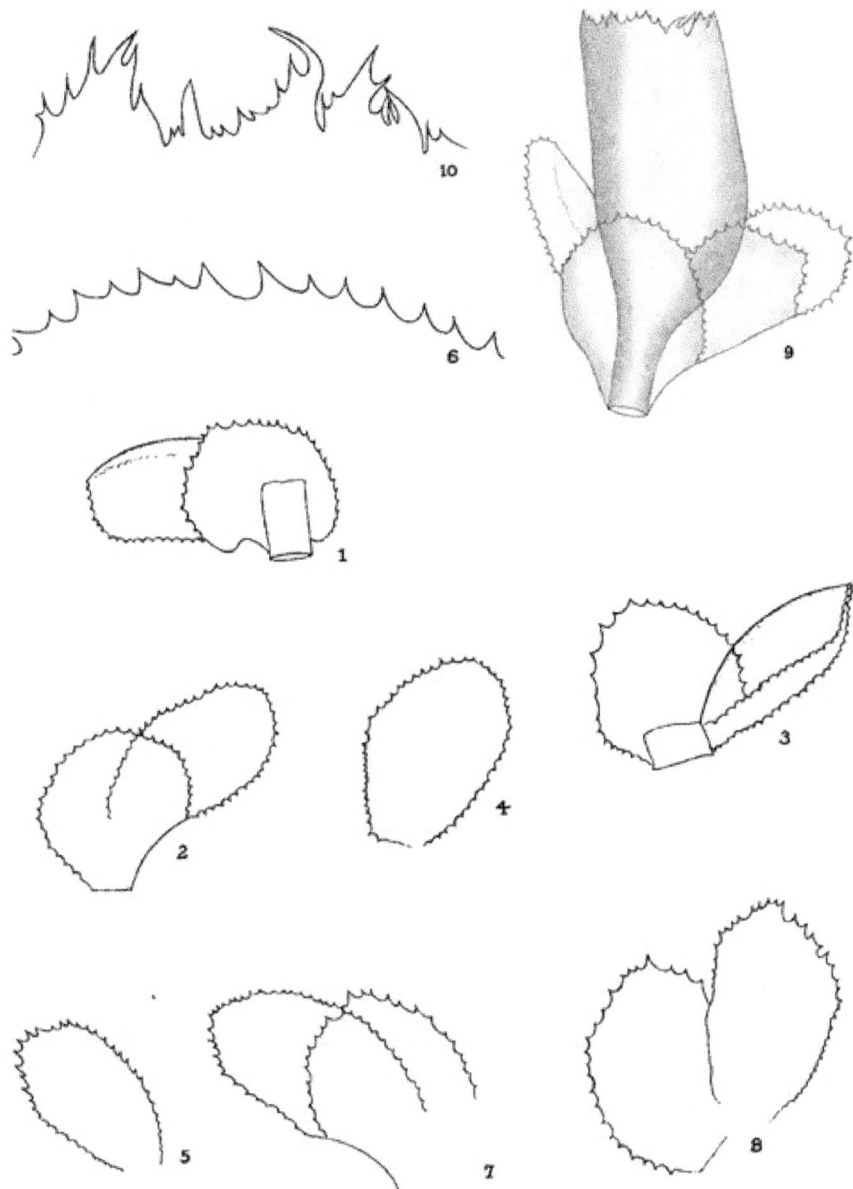

W. H. P. del.

Mortimer & Co. Lith.

Scapania Bolanderi

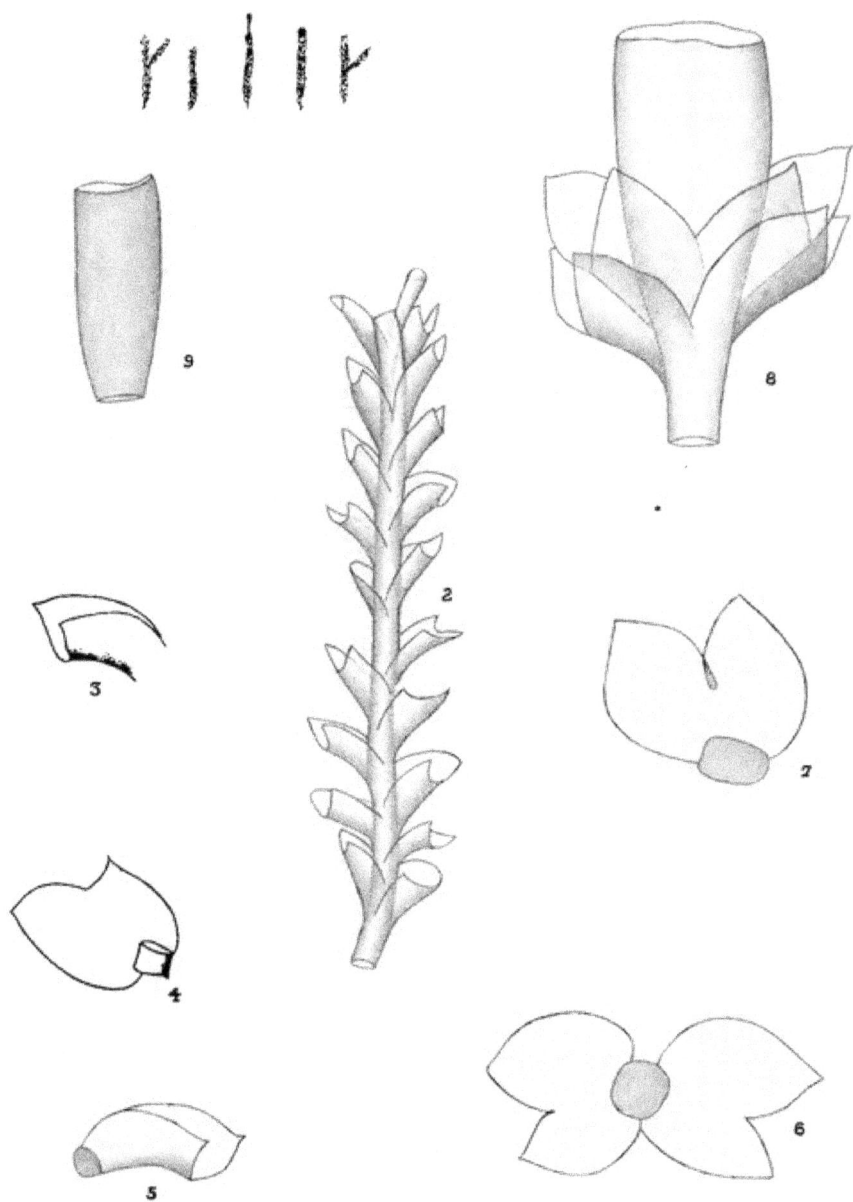

W. H. P. del.

Mortimer & Co. Lith.

Scapania glaucocephala.

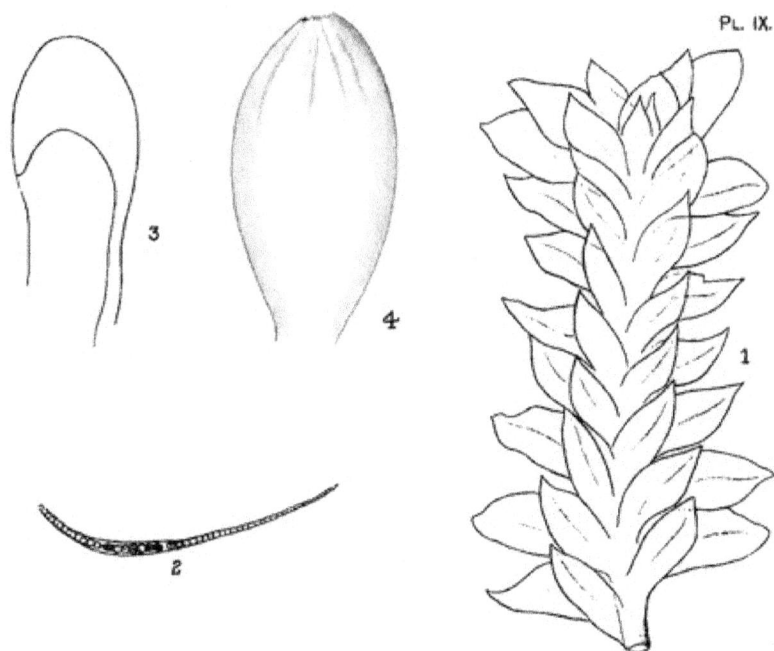

Diplophyllum albicans.

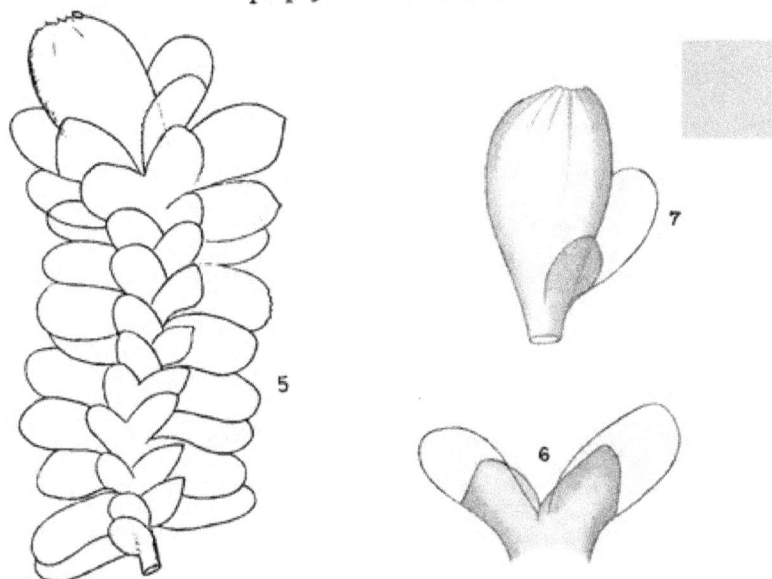

W. H. P., del.

Martimer & Co. Lith.

Diplophyllum taxifolium.

PL. X.

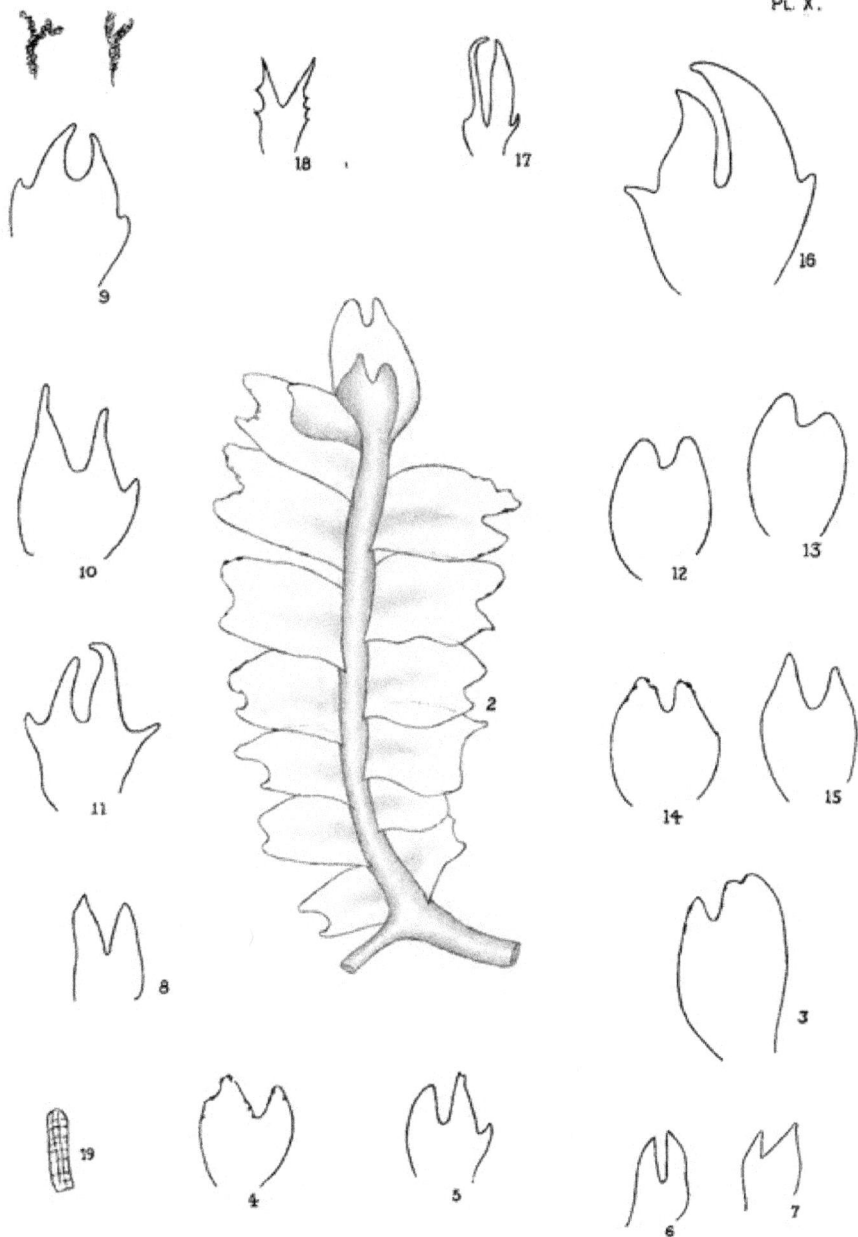

W. H. P. del.

Mortimer & Co. Lith.

Lophocolea minor.

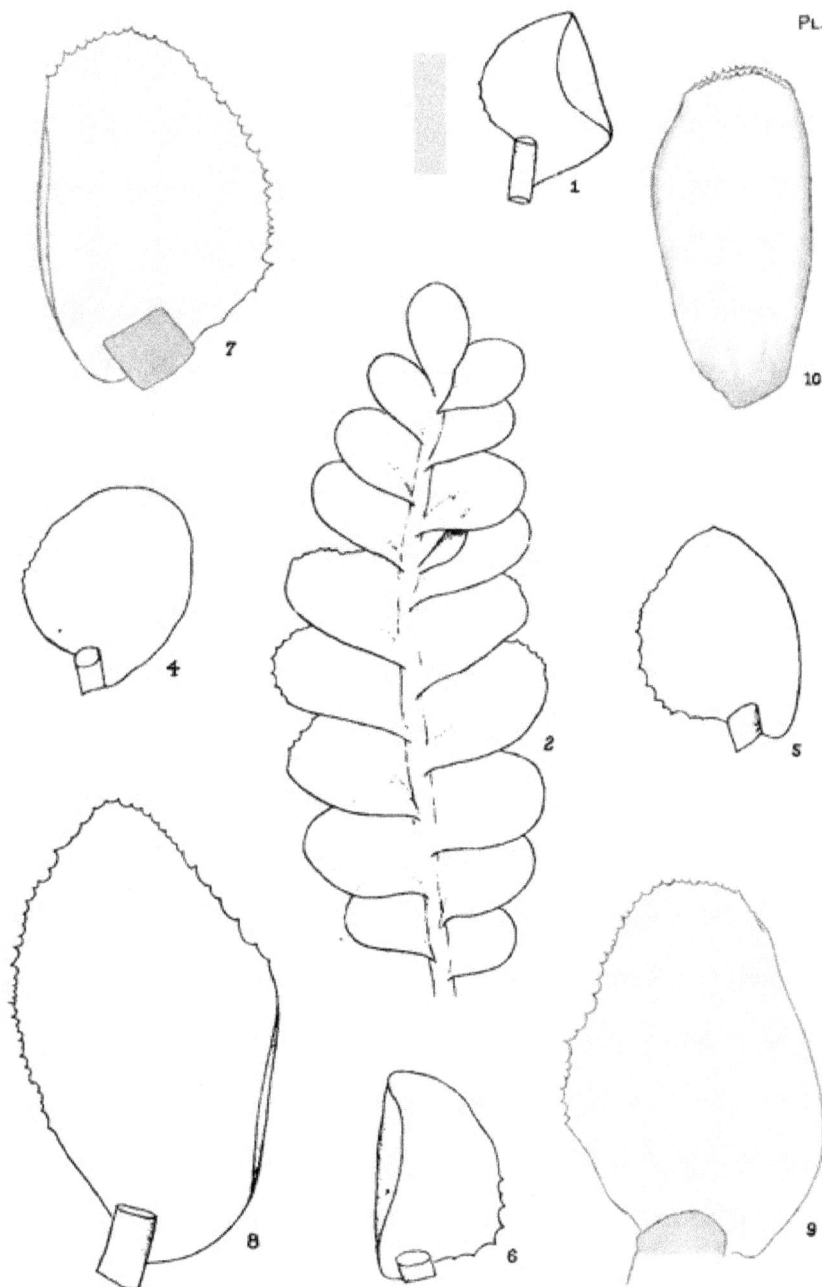

W. H. P, del.

Mortimer & Co. Lith.

Plagiochila porelloides.

Pl. XII.

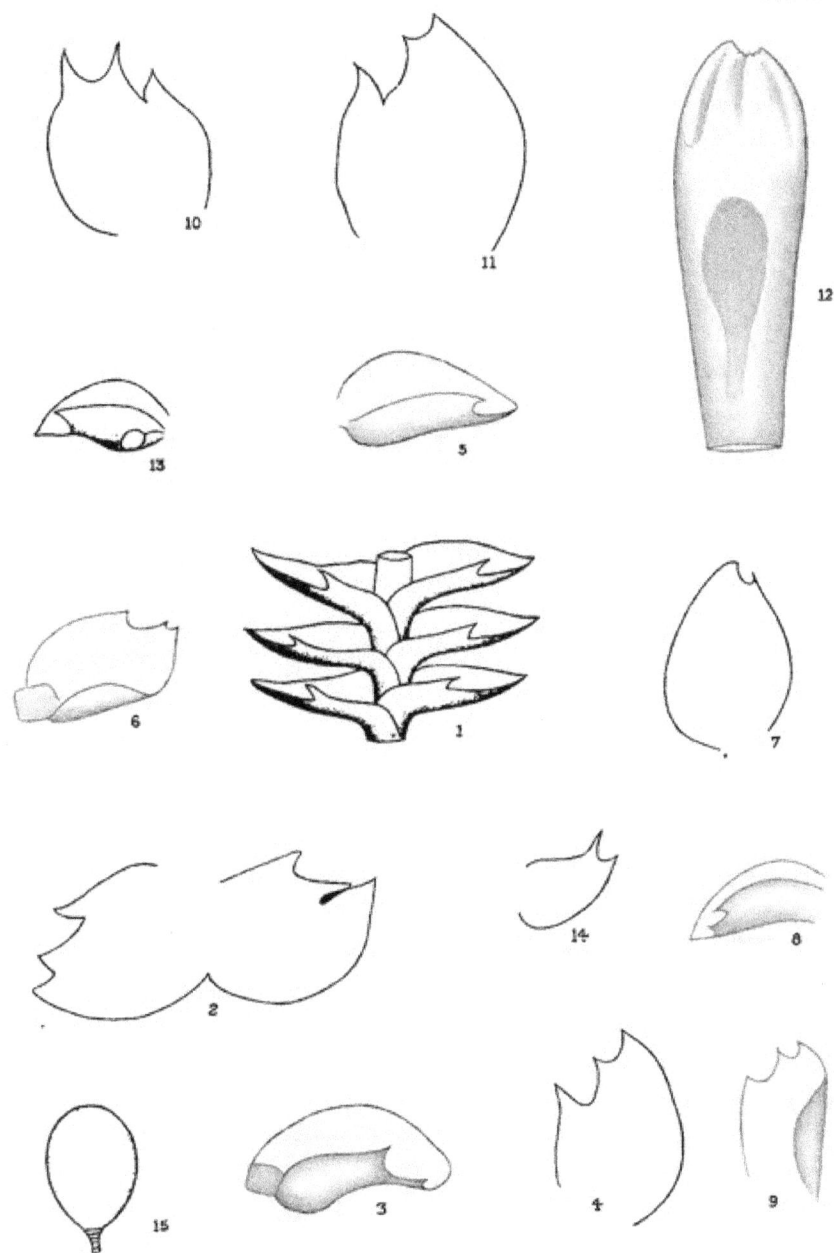

W. H. P. del.

Mortimer & Co. Lith.

Jungermania exsecta.

INDEX.

www.ingramcontent.com/pod-product-compliance
Lightning Source LLC
Chambersburg PA
CBHW031752090426
42739CB00008B/979